Violence and Marxism
Marx to Mao

Violence and Marxism

Marx to Mao

Rustam Singh

Violence and Marxism: Marx to Mao

by Rustam Singh

First Published, 2015

ISBN: 978-93-5002-371-6 (Hb)

Published by

Aakar Books

28 E, Pocket IV, Mayur Vihar Phase I, Delhi-110091
Phone: o11-22795505 Telefax: 011-22795641
aakarbooks@gmail.com
www.aakarbooks.com

Printed at:
Sapra Brothers, Delhi-110092

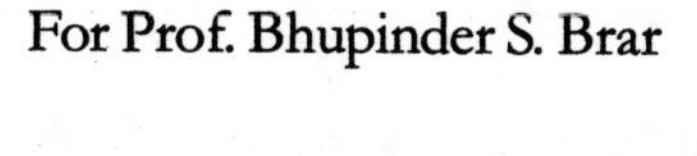

For Prof. Bhupinder S. Brar

Contents

Preface

This book is a part of an ongoing project on the phenomenon of violence. The latest outcome of that project is my paper "Roots of Violence: *Jîva*, Life and Other Things".[1] However, the very first outcome of the project was my M.Phil. dissertation on "The Status of Violence in Marx's Theory of Revolution",[2] which developed, a few years later, into my Ph.D. thesis, "Status of Violence in the Marxist Theory of Revolution: From Marx to Mao".[3] This book is based on, and is an updated version of, that thesis.

Reading the thesis now I felt that this topic remains as relevant today as it was when the thesis was written. Secondly, when I wrote the thesis it was the only book-length study on this topic and, so far as I am aware, it remains so even today. Finally, some of the people who have read parts of this study that were published as papers have been suggesting over the years that I publish it as a book so that it becomes fully and more widely available.

I have made some changes in the text—including in the Introduction where I have mentioned the work related to this topic done after I had submitted my thesis. However, such changes are not many. This is so because, going over the relevant statements of Marx, Engels, Lenin and Mao—the thinkers whose views I have elaborated and interpreted in this book—and the circumstances under which they made these statements, I did not feel that I needed to make any drastic amendment in my understanding of these statements.

Most of the changes that I have made are in the last chapter, the Conclusion, where, apart from doing some other things, I have removed those portions, paragraphs or sentences which referred to certain economic and political developments—in Europe, Asia, Africa and Latin America—that had taken place or were still taking place when I wrote the thesis. I now believe that the study, being a purely interpretative work, could have done without such references.

It is for this same reason that I have not made any attempt, even now at this moment when the study is being published, to analyse any contemporary violent political movements of Marxist orientation in the light of my findings—such as the Naxalite or the so-called Maoist movement currently going on in India—something that was suggested to me by some quarters. I believe that such a task does not fall within the ambit of this work which is essentially an exercise in textual analysis.

In any case, that task cannot be undertaken as an appendage of this work: if at all, it needs to be done as an independent work and may run into more than one book-length analysis. It goes without saying, nevertheless, that an analysis of that nature, if it is serious in its intent, will need to consult, in fact inevitably depend upon, a study like this.

***

The thesis on which this book is based was written under the capable supervision of my teacher Prof. Bhupinder S. Brar who gave me a lot of freedom to draw my inferences and conclusions but at the same time cautioned me whenever I tended to go too far away from what the texts would allow. My debt to him is deep and abiding. I am also indebted and must show my deep respect to Prof. K. K. Pathak who was a constant source of encouragement and who always goaded me to finish my work whenever he felt I was wavering. Prof. Randhir Singh and Prof. Sudipta Kaviraj read parts of that thesis and made favourable comments. I'm grateful to them.

Finally, I must thank the editorial staff of *Economic and Political Weekly*, Mumbai, which carried portions of this book in earlier versions, as has been mentioned in the notes below.

Rustam Singh

NOTES

[1] See, Saitya Brata Das and Soumyabrata Choudhury, eds., *The Weight of Violence: Religion, Language, Politics*, Oxford University Press, New Delhi, 2015, pp. 169-82.

[2] A paper based on this dissertation, under the same title, had appeared in *Economic and Political Weekly* in their issue of January 28, 1989.

[3] Another paper, this time based on the Ph.D. thesis, namely "Violence in the Leninist Revolution", had appeared, again, in *Economic and Political Weekly* (December 29, 1990).

Introduction

The aim of this study is to comprehend the status of violence in the Marxist theory of revolution. In more specific terms, our task involves finding answers to the following questions: Is the Marxist revolution necessarily violent, or have the leading Marxist thinkers and activists admitted the possibility of a peaceful transformation as well? What are, if at all there are any, the circumstances under which peaceful transformation may take place? Is the violent or peaceful nature of the revolution determined by the very structures of a given society? If so, is it determined solely by the economic structures? Or, do political structures too have a role to play? To what extent can the role of these structures be independent of the economic structures? Does the level of capitalist economic development affect the nature of the revolution, making it violent or peaceful? That is to say, will the nature of the revolution be different if the capitalist economic structures are less, or more, developed at a given place? What about the place where capitalist development has just begun but where a Marxist revolution is contemplated? Similarly, does the predominantly feudal character of a society have something to do with the violent or peaceful nature of the revolution? Further, once the revolution is violent, is the degree of violence determined by such factors? Do international factors too play some role in making the revolution violent or peaceful? If so, what is the nature of these factors, how do they operate, and under what kinds of circumstances? Do the leading Marxist thinkers admit of the role of conscious subjective intervention in the process of revolution? If so, what impact is it most likely to have on the nature of the revolution in the aforementioned terms? What are the conditions under which such intervention is acceptable? Finally, to what extent, if at all, and why, did the later Marxist thinkers deviate from the original Marxian position over this issue? Were there any differences among these later thinkers? If so, what were these differences, and what were the reasons for them?

The usefulness of the present study should lie in the fact that the issue of violence in the Marxist revolution has remained a subject of unresolved controversy. The controversy has spanned both the theoretical and practical fields of the world communist movement. In both these fields, it has been a major divisive issue, and has led, at different stages of the movement, to the adoption and propagation of conflicting and contradictory strategies at the domestic as well as at the international level.

Controversy

The controversy first gained prominence after the death of Engels (1895) and lasted, in this form, till the end of the Second International (1889-1914). Among those who participated in this debate were such leading socialist theoreticians of the period as Eduard Bernstein, Karl Kautsky and Rosa Luxemburg. The point at issue was whether capitalism had to be overthrown and socialism established through violent struggle, or could this be achieved through peaceful means by using to the advantages of the working class the political institutions of the bourgeois state? The answer to this problem involved accepting or rejecting participation in bourgeois parliamentary politics. If this participation was accepted, it raised the further question of the degree of this participation. To what extent could a Marxist party get involved in bourgeois parliamentary politics without compromising its revolutionary aims and principles?

Bernstein, Kautsky and Rosa Luxemburg, all provided different answers to these questions, suggesting diverging strategies and tactics.

Kautsky and Luxemburg quoted Marx and Engels to 'prove' their respective cases. Not so Bernstein who argued that there was no need for the working class to wage a violent struggle to capture political power in order to transform capitalism into socialism. The living standards of the working class were rising. A new middle class had developed, and was expanding. Alongside these developments had emerged parliamentary democratic institutions. These had become so deeply entrenched that the ruling bourgeoisie could not, at will, manipulate them against working class interests.[1]

Kautsky challenged Bernstein's thesis that capitalism would get transformed into socialism without a violent struggle. This struggle, he contended, was inevitable as there was a basic class contradiction between the bourgeoisie and the proletariat. The contradiction did not disappear because of the development of capitalism. On the contrary, it got increasingly sharpened as capitalism matured. The sharpening of the contradiction led to an intensification of the class struggle which had to end, finally, in a violent capture of political power by the working class. However, the working class could capture power only when the conditions were ripe. Therefore, till the conditions became ripe the workers' parties must engage themselves in the struggle for democratic reforms within capitalism.[2]

Rosa Luxemburg agreed with Kautsky that the proletariat could not win power and bring about socialism without a violent struggle. But this struggle, according to her, had to be launched immediately. Accepting struggle for reforms as a form of political activity meant acceptance of bourgeois rule for an indefinite period because reforms, as an activity, were typical of bourgeois democracy. Therefore, the working class must not wait for the conditions to ripen before taking violent action for capturing power. This action itself was necessary to make the conditions ripe. It could not be postponed till a future date.[3]

The Sino-Soviet Split

The second occasion on which the controversy acquired prominence was towards the later half of the 1950s. It became, by the early 1960s, a major cause of a sharp division in the world communist movement along the lines of what has come to be known as the Sino-Soviet split. The issues, this time, were: (1) What form, violent or peaceful, should the revolutions take in both the developed capitalist and the ex-colonial underdeveloped countries? (2) What stance should the international communist movement in general and the socialist countries in particular adopt towards the above-mentioned revolutions? In other words, should it be a stance of active, militant collaboration, or one of mere ideological support? We can see that the controversy assumed slightly different form this time. Firstly, the debate took place between the leaderships of two (socialist) countries, and not among Marxist thinkers as such. And secondly, whereas the earlier debate focused on matters of strategy and tactics primarily at the domestic level, the new debate encompassed the international level as well. The reason for this obviously was the changed international situation in which the world communist movement now found itself.

Evoking the authority of Lenin, the Soviets contended that violence and civil war were not "the only way to remake society".[4] According to them, the contemporary historical situation offered the working class "in a number of capitalist and former colonial countries" an opportunity "to capture a stable majority in Parliament", and "to secure the transfer of the basic means of production into the hands of the people". However, in countries where capitalism was "still strong", and had "a huge military and police apparatus at its disposal", the transition to socialism was still to "be attended by a sharp class, revolutionary struggle".[5] On the basis of this argument, the Soviets concluded that there was no need of "armed interference by the socialist countries" in the countries where capitalism still existed.[6]

The Chinese did not reject the Soviet thesis outright, but they did not agree with it either. They asserted, in Lenin's words, that the possibility of attaining power and carrying out transition to socialism by peaceful means was "extraordinarily rare".[7] They quoted Lenin to claim, first, that "No ruling class in the world ever gave way without a struggle", and second, that "The reactionary classes themselves are usually the first to resort to violence, to civil war".[8] This being the case, it was "difficult to imagine" that the proletariat could adopt measures in parliament for a "peaceful transition to socialism" just because it had won "a certain number of votes in parliament". Therefore, the communists should "take part in parliamentary struggles", but they should have "no illusions"[9] about the bourgeois parliamentary system. It was true, the Chinese said, that the rise of socialism at the world level had "weakened the position of the imperialist violence in the world".[10] But this was not sufficient to prevent the imperialists from oppressing the people in individual countries. Therefore, "people everywhere should give their support" to "the anti-imperialist struggles".[11]

A point that emerges from the above exposition is that the question whether according to the Marxist doctrine a peaceful transition to socialism is possible assumed increasing significance over the years. The debate on this question revolved mainly around the bourgeois parliamentary institutions. Although there were attempts to play down the importance of these institutions, their strategic and tactical implications for the communist movement could be ignored by none. After the collapse of 'socialism' in countries where it was brought about or imposed through violent means, albeit in the absence of parliamentary institutions, this question has become all the more relevant. The resolution of this question, one way or another, will determine, to a large extent, the further course of the communist movement. It is also going to affect, in a significant manner, the domestic politics especially of the 'developing' capitalist or semi-capitalist societies where the communist parties are active.

Yet the question has never received the kind of attention it deserves. The literature dealing with the subject is extremely meagre. To the best of our knowledge, systematic, detailed and comprehensive discussion focusing exclusively on this subject has not been attempted in the past. There are, of course, some works which engage with the issue of violence in the Marxist theory. But, firstly, this engagement is either marginal or partial. In other words, it occurs either as part of a larger discussion of a particular Marxist thinker[12] or as discussion of any one of his works.[13] Where the discussion focuses exclusively on violence, it deals with only one thinker.[14] When the discussion extends to more than one thinker, it is extremely brief.[15] Occasionally, a specific aspect of violence, for example terrorism, has been taken up and examined in detail.[16]

As the title of this study makes clear, we are carrying our discussion only up to Mao. The thinkers we are including in addition to Marx and Mao are Engels and Lenin. Why have we chosen for discussion only the thinkers that we have? For the simple reason that others have either not reserved a major place for violence in their theory and strategy of revolution, or they have done so without providing sufficient justification for the same. Regis Debray and Che Guevara, especially, fall in this latter category. They have taken a violent revolution for granted and have gone ahead devising a viable strategy for it, practically ignoring the theoretical issues. Others like Leon Trotsky and Rosa Luxemburg have been excised because although they accepted the necessity of a violent revolution in principle, they did not devote much space to this theme in their writings. There are still others like Herbert Marcuse and Slavoj Žižek who could have been included had their views on revolutionary violence been incontrovertibly accepted as Marxist.

Methodology

We shall now make a couple of clarifications regarding the methodology we plan to adopt for this work.

As is known, the single most important contribution to the Marxist theory of revolution has been that of Marx and Engels. The other and the later contributions are in the nature of additions to or alterations of this theory, although this in no way diminishes their importance. This means that a major portion of our study will be devoted to examining the views of Marx and Engels, and that the other thinkers, namely Lenin and Mao, will be discussed in the background of what they had already pronounced.

Secondly, whereas Marx and Engels were primarily thinkers, both Lenin and Mao were primarily activists who engaged themselves in theoretical exercise in order to clarify and solve the immediate questions of strategy and tactics. Apart from this, the views of all these thinkers, starting with Marx himself, evolved over time, and kept changing according to the needs of the proletarian movement in which all of them were active participants. This was particularly true of their views on the issue of violence. This being so, the format of our study must primarily be historical and chronological. In other words, we will have to examine not only the views of these thinkers but also the specific historical conditions in which these views took shape.

NOTES

[1] See David McLellan, *Marxism After Marx: An Introduction*, Macmillan, London & Basingstoke, 1979, pp. 30-31; Lucio Colletti, *From Rousseau to Lenin: Studies in Ideology and Society*, Oxford University Press, New Delhi, 1978, pp. 50-51; Leszek Kolakowski, *Main Currents of Marxism, Volume II*, Clarendon Press, Oxford, 1978, pp. 105-06; G. D. H. Cole, *The Second International, 1889-1914, Part I*, Macmillan, London, 1963, pp. 263-90; Julius Braunthal, *History of the International, 1864-1914*, Thomas Nelson and Sons, London, 1966, p. 263.

[2] See McLellan, ibid., pp. 31-33; Kolakowski, ibid., pp. 43-50; Cole, ibid., pp. 267-71.

[3] See McLellan, ibid., pp. 42-45; Kolakowski, ibid., pp. 61, 66 and 76-77; and Paul Mattick, *Anti-Bolshevik Communism*, Merlin Press, London, 1978, pp. 21-22.

[4] N. Khrushchev's Twentieth Congress Speech. Extracts in G. F. Hudson et al, *The Sino-Soviet Dispute*, The China Quarterly, London, 1961, p. 45.

[5] Ibid., p. 46.

[6] Ibid., pp. 42-43. See also, Bhupinder Singh Brar, "The Sino-Soviet Split and the Indian Communist Movement", unpublished Ph.D. thesis, Jawaharlal Nehru University, New Delhi, 1983, pp. 83-91.

[7] See the article, "Long Live Leninism", *Peoples' Daily*, April 16, 1960. Text in Hudson et al, op. cit., p. 103.

[8] Ibid., p. 101.

[9] Ibid., p. 107.

[10] Ibid., p. 95.

[11] See Yu Chao-li, "Imperialism—Source of War in Modern Times—and the Path of the Peoples' Struggle for Peace", *Peking Review*, No. 15 (1960). Quoted in Hudson et al, ibid., p. 81. See also, Bhupinder Singh Brar, op. cit., pp. 91-101.

[12] See, for example, Richard W. Miller, *Analyzing Marx: Morality, Power and History*, Princeton University Press, Princeton, 1984, pp. 114-26, for Marx; Marcel Liebman, *Leninism Under Lenin*, Merlin Press, London, 1980, pp. 165-80, and Bertram D. Wolfe, "Leninism", in Milorad M. Drachkovitch, ed., *Marxism in the Modern World*, Stanford University Press, Stanford, 1973, pp. 68-73, for Lenin; and Arthur A. Cohen, *The Communism of Mao Tse-tung*, The University of Chicago Press, Chicago and London, 1964, pp. 105-15 and 126-38, for Mao.

[13] See Lucio Colletti, op. cit., pp. 219-27. Here such comments occur during a discussion of Lenin's *The State and Revolution*.

[14] See James Ryan, *Lenin's Terror: The Ideaological Origins of Early Soviet State Violence*, Routledge, London and Abingdon, 2014. However, it should be noted that Ryan's book is concerned more with the origins of the violence perpetrated by the Soviet state in its early years than with Lenin's entire theory of violence.

[15] See Christopher J. Finlay, "Violence and Revolutionary Subjectivity: Marx to Žižek", UCD Geary Discussion Paper Series, January 11, 2006. http://www.ucd.ie/geary/static/publications/workingpapers/GearyWp200601.pdf. Accessed on May 30, 2015.

[16] See Shlomo Avineri, *The Social and Political Thought of Karl Marx*, S. Chand & Company, New Delhi, 1977, Chapter 7, for a discussion on terrorism in Marx.

1

Violent Revolution and the Possibility of Peaceful Change

The issue of violence has been treated in the Marxist theory at broadly two distinct levels. At the first, general, level the discussion is largely theoretical. This discussion, initiated mainly by Marx and Engels but also contributed to by others, concludes that the nature of the revolution in bourgeois societies will be inevitably violent. This nature of the revolution, as per this argument, is determined by the nature and historical development of the bourgeois economic and political structures and institutions.

At the second, more specific, level the discussion is comparatively unorganised and fragmented, and is based primarily on the practical political experiences of the thinkers under consideration—those of Marx and Engels in western Europe, of Lenin in tsarist Russia, and of Mao in feudal and colonial China. Inevitably, therefore, whereas at the first level the discussion deals with only the bourgeois societies, and that too in a largely abstracted manner, the latter discussion takes into account the specific peculiarities of each society. Inevitably, too, this discussion branches out into different directions and arrives at different conclusions at the hands of different thinkers.

In the present chapter, we will explicate the relatively more pervasive theoretical arguments for the inevitably violent nature of revolution in bourgeois societies as well as the somewhat paradoxical alternate view, also held more or less simultaneously by Marx and Engels, that a peaceful revolution too was indeed possible in bourgeois-democratic societies.

Inevitability of Violence

At the general theoretical level, Marx and Engels believed that a violent socialist revolution was inevitable. The inevitability of the violent nature of the revolution was determined by the very structures of the bourgeois society and their histroical development. Marx and Engels concluded this on the basis of their analysis of historical forces and the then existing social relations, and of the nature of private property.

According to Marx and Engels, during the course of their development a stage comes when the productive forces "are no longer productive but destructive forces", and become the cause of a "mischief" under the "existing relations". This is the period of the rule of a particular class of society which derives its power from its property and whose rule finds its expression in the form of the state. This is also the period of the existence of another class which forms the majority of the members of a society. This second class "has to bear the burden of society without enjoying its advantages". These conditions lead the oppressed class to acquire the consciousness of the necessity of a "fundamental revolution". This consciousness culminates in the revolutionary struggle directed against the class till then in power, and aims at overthrowing the existing "mode of activity". Marx and Engels here emphasise not only the inevitability but also the necessity of revolution. "The revolution is necessary…not only because the ruling class cannot be overthrown in any other way, but also because the class overthrowing it can only in a revolution succeed in ridding itself of all the muck of ages and become fitted to found society anew".[1]

These contending classes in the capitalist society are the bourgeoisie and the proletariat. The proletariat, as the oppressed class, is the particular product of the capitalist phase of the historical development. The historical mission of the proletariat is to emancipate itself from this oppression. The working class cannot emancipate itself unless it abolishes all classes. This abolition will take the form of class struggle between the bourgeoisie and the proletariat, and will culminate, as Marx puts it, in "total revolution", "the shock of body against body". This 'total revolution', this 'shock of body against body' is inevitable, for the end of a society founded on the oppositon of classes is a "brutal contradiction". Thus, till a new society emerges in which there are no longer any classes and no class antagonisms, "on the eve of every general reshuffling of society, the last word of social science will always be: 'combat or death, bloody struggle or extinction…'"[2]

Private Property

The struggle between the bourgeoisie and the proletariat revolves round the institution of private property, which itself is a product of historical forces. Private property acts as an instrument in the hands of these forces.[3] But it also plays an autonomous role in this struggle, a role that independently determines the inevitability of the violent nature of the revolution. This role springs from the peculiar nature of private property.

The nature of private property, according to Marx and Engels, is such that in its compulsion to maintain itself into existence it has to maintain the existence also of the proletariat, which is its opposite and its own product. The nature of the proletariat, on the other hand, is such that it is compelled to abolish its opposite and its creator, the private property. There is, thus, a contradiction between private property and the proletariat. This contradiction drives private property towards its own destruction, and the proletariat becomes the instrument of this destruction.[4]

The point to be noted here is that in essence it is not only the proletariat that abolishes private property. Rather, it is also the private property that abolishes itself, since its abolition lies in its very effort to perpetuate itself. But that does not mean that the end of private property will come on its own, without the proletariat. The argument is just the opposite. The end of private property will come only through the proletariat, for the proletariat and the "inhuman"[5] conditions under which it is forced to live are the essential product of private property. These conditions drive the proletariat to "revolt"[6] against the world of private property. This revolt culminates in the "action of annihilating"[7] this world. Hence the inevitability of the violent nature of the revolution.

Growth of the Bourgeoisie

Tracing the growth of the bourgeoisie during and after the feudal era, Marx and Engels show how it comes to acquire political domination. "Each step in the development of the bourgeoisie was accompanied by a corresponding political advance of that class". The process continued till at last, with the establishment of the modern industry and the world market, the bourgeoisie "conquered for itself, in the modern representative state, exclusive political sway."[8]

In the meantime, with the growth of industry the proletariat increases in number; it also becomes concentrated in large masses and its strength grows. The growing impoverishment of the workers and the precariousness of their existence compel them to adopt a confrontational course against the bourgeoisie, and thus their struggle against the latter starts. First, the fight is carried on at individual level, but soon it acquires the character of a collision between the two classes. Thus, the struggle becomes a political struggle, for every class struggle, according to Marx and Engels, "is a political struggle".[9] This struggle of the proletariat against the bourgeoisie is the result of its conditions of existence, conditions which are determined by the bourgeois order itself. The bourgeois order itself, therefore, is responsible for forging the workers into a class and then furnishing them "with weapons for fighting the bourgeoisie".[10] It produces, in other words, "its own grave diggers".[11]

The struggle of the proletariat against the bourgeoisie is, thus, inevitable. Equally inevitable will be the violent nature of this struggle. For the aim of the struggle will inevitably be to demolish the bourgeois mode of production and, thereby, the bourgeois social order which stands on its shoulders. All the preceding classes that ruled the society gained their dominant position "by subjecting the society at large to their conditions of appropriation". The proletarians, too, "cannot become the masters of the productive forces of society...cannot raise themselves up, without the whole superincumbent strata of official society being sprung into the air". Having nothing of their own to secure, "their mission is to destroy all previous securities for, and insurances of, individual property". The struggle rages within the bourgeois society as a "veiled civil war" up to a point and then "breaks out into open revolution", culminating in "the violent overthrow of the bourgeoisie".[12]

Lenin and Mao

So far as the substance of the above argument is concerned, neither Lenin nor Mao add much by way of theoretical analysis of the bourgeois structures and their historical development. But one can observe some shift of emphasis alright. According to Lenin, "In the final analysis", it was force alone that settled "the great problems of political liberty and the class struggle".[13] It was "most probable...that the bourgeoisie will not make peaceful concessions to the proletariat and at the decisive moment will resort to violence for the defence of its privileges. In that case no other way will be left to the proletariat for the achievement of its own aim but that of revolution."[14]

Rather than emphasising directly the structures of the bourgeois society and the historical form that they adopt, Lenin points out the tendency of the bourgeoisie not to give up its power peacefully which will make a violent proletarian revolution inevitable as well as necessary.

This, too, was essentially the argument of Mao. As early as 1920-21, he wrote: "...no despot, imperialist and militarist...has ever been known to leave the stage of history of his own free will without being overthrown by the people". Mao wrote this in response to what Bertrand Russell, the English philosopher, had said during his tour of China in these years. Denouncing the violent methods of the communists, Russell had argued that they could attain their goal through education and persuasion.[15] In two letters Mao wrote at the time to his friend Ts'ai Ho-Sen, he objected to Russell's veiwpoint. "This is all very well as a theory", he wrote, "but it is unfeasible in practice". In the present-day world, the schools and the press, "the two most important instruments of education", were "entirely under the capitalist control". The capitalists also had parliaments to pass laws protecting their interests, governments to apply these laws, and police and army to enforce them and "to repress the demands of the proletariat". In addition, they had factories through which they "monopolised the production of goods, and banks to serve as repositories in the circulation of their wealth". Under such circumstances, one could not overthrow capitalism "by the force of a few feeble efforts in the domain of education". Having "a mouth" and "a tongue" and a few schools and newspapers "as means of propaganda" was "not really enough".[16]

Similarly, in 1957, disagreeing with Khrushchev on the question of peaceful transition, Mao maintained: "…the bourgeoisie will never hand over state power of their own accord, but will resort to violence". A communist party, according to him, could surely adopt the slogan of peaceful transition as a "defensive" and "tactical" weapon. This would show that this party wanted peace not war. It would help the party "to win over the masses" and gain "initiative". But this slogan had no greater significance than this. Therefore, the "strategic slogan" must always remain: "To seize state power by armed force".[17]

Earlier, in November 1938, Mao had described "the seizure of power by armed force" as the "central task and the highest form of revolution". It was in this context that he had written his famous sentence: "Political power grows out of the barrel of a gun". Continuing in the same vein, he had added : "Experience in the class struggle in the era of imperialism teaches us that it is only by the power of the gun that the working class and the labouring masses can defeat the armed bourgeoisie and the landlords; in this sense we may say that only with guns can the whole world be transformed."[18]

The above argument can in sum be stated as follows. The nature of the bourgeois economic structures is inherently exploitative. The political institutions that develop over these structures are, therefore, necessarily oppressive. The historical development of these structures and institutions makes them even more exploitative and oppressive. These facts and developments result in the increasing deterioration in the material conditions of the working class. These conditions force the workers to acquire political and revolutionary consciousness, and they start organising themselves with the aim of getting rid of these conditions. But because of the concentration of economic and political power in the hands of the bourgeoisie, the structures and institutions that produce these conditions cannot be gotten rid of peacefully. Therefore, the working class is forced to overthrow the bourgeoisie through a violent revolution.

The Alternate View

Lenin and Mao continued to believe throughout their lives in the theoretical position brought out above. Marx and Engels, too, did not give up this position.[19] Nevertheless, elements of an alternate view always existed in a subdued manner in their writings and pronouncements. This view, which assumed slightly more concrete shape in later years, holds indications of an almost complete reversal of their theory of an inevitably violent revolution in bourgeois societies. However, this view was not adequately developed or integrated with the first view, with the result that they continued to hold these two nearly opposite views simultaneously, thus introducing an unresolved conflict in their theory of violence.

We will now outline the development of this alternate view in the writings and pronouncements of Marx and Engels. In addition, we will elaborate certain ideas of Lenin and Mao which would reinforce their position brought out above and would underline, at the same time, their total disagreement with the alternate view of Marx and Engels mentioned above.

The Peaceful Course

Hints of the alternate view that emerged more unambiguously in early 1850s onwards can be seen in some of the earlier statements of Engels. In *Principles of Communism*, written at the end of 1847, Engels asked himself the question: Will it be possible to bring about the abolition of private property by peaceful methods? (Question 16) and gave the following answer:

> It is to be desired that this could happen, and Communists certainly would be the last to resist it. The Communists know only too well that all conspiracies are not only futile but even harmful. They know only too well that revolutions are not made deliberately and arbitrarily, but that everywhere and at all times they are the essential outcome of circumstances quite independent of the will and the leadership of particular parties and entire classes. But they like-wise perceive that the development of the proletariat is in nearly every civilised country forcibly suppressed, and that thereby the opponents of the Communists are tending in every way to promote revolution. Should the oppressed proletariat in the end be goaded into a revolution, we Communists will then defend the cause of the proletarians by deed just as well as we do now by word.[20]

Engels' answer is self-explanatory. We can see that even in these early years he was not averse to the idea of peaceful change. In fact, he wished that such a thing were possible. But since changes are brought about by circumstances, therefore if the circumstances are such that they rule out the possibility of a peaceful change, then the change had to be violent. For example, if the proletarians' efforts for change are forcibly suppressed, as Engels says was being done in all 'civilised' countries during his time, then they will be "goaded into a revolution", that is, they will be forced to resort to violent methods of bringing change.

That Engels was not opposed to the notion of peaceful change is further confirmed from what he had said in a speech in Elberfeld on February 15, 1845. After outlining the inevitability of a violent upheaval, he had made the following remarks:

> If, gentlemen, these conclusions are correct, if the social revolution and practical communism are the necessary result of our existing conditions—then we will have to concern

> ourselves above all with the measures by which we can avoid a violent and bloody overthrow of the social conditions. And there is only one means, namely, the peaceful introduction of communism. If we do not want the bloody solution of the social problem...then, gentlemen, we must apply oursevles seriously and without prejudice to the social problem, then we must make it our business to contribute our share towards humanising the condition of the modern helots.[21]

It could seem that by "humanising the condition of the modern helots" or by "peaceful introduction of communism" Engels meant reforms within the bourgeois order. What puts this interpretation into doubt is Marx's and Engels' analysis of the bourgeois order that we have seen earlier and as per which revolution and communism were the necessary result of the bourgeois social conditions. If this was so, then there was no question of suggesting reforms within the bourgeois order, for this would imply perpetuation of this order. Engels' remarks could only mean that social revolution could be made to take a peaceful instead of the violent course it would normally take. But what the exact nature of this course would be Engels does not as yet outline.

Universal Suffrage

The likely nature of the peaceful revolution was for the first time indicated by Marx in 1852. In an article published in the *New York Daily Tribune* on August 25, he wrote:

> Universal suffrage is the equivalent of political power for the working class of England, where the proletariat forms the majority of the population and where, in a long, though underground civil war, it has gained a clear consciousness of its position as a class...The carrying of Universal Suffrage in England would, therefore, be a far more socialistic measure

> than anythig which has been honoured with that name on the continent.
>
> Its inevitable result, here, is the *political supremacy of the working class.*[22]

Marx here points out the difference between the British and the continental conditions, and hints at the possibility of a peaceful transfer of power to the working class in Britain through universal suffrage. However, the statement does not clearly spell out whether the existence of universal suffrage would necessarily mean an abandonment of the violent methods of struggle.

Marx made a similarly ambiguous statement in September 1871 when the London Conference of the First International passed a resolution declaring its commitment to normal political activity, as against the Bakuninists who favoured only direct political action. Supporting the resolution, Marx said: "...the governments are opposed to us: we must answer them with all the means that are at our disposal...We must declare to the governments: we will proceed against you peaceably where it is possible and by force of arms when it may be necessary".[23] Although Marx made this statement in order to oppose the anarchist position against ordinary political activity, yet the statement can lend itself to conflictng interpretations. Read in the light of his statement of 1852 quoted earlier, the statement seems to mean that when Marx tells the governments that "we will proceed against you peaceably where it is possible", it is the possibility of a peaceful capture of power through universal suffrage that he has in mind here too.

But this position of Marx gets confirmed only in 1872 when, immediately after the Hague Congress of the First International, he made the following remarks in a speech at Amsterdam on September 8:

> The workers will some day have to win supermacy in order to organise labour along new lines…
>
> But we have by no means affirmed that the goal would be achieved by identical means.
>
> We know of the allowances we must make for the institutions, customs and traditions of the various countries, and we do not deny that there are countries such as America, England, and I would add Holland if I knew your institutions better, where the working people may achieve their goal by peaceful means.[24]

Earlier, in an interview, published in the American journal *Woodhull and Claflin's Weekly*, on August 12, 1871, Marx had remarked: "In England…the way is open for the working class to develop their political power. In a place where they can achieve their goal more quickly and more securely through peaceful propaganda, insurrection would be a folly".[25]

Here Marx confirms in unambiguous terms what he had earlier only hinted at: political institutions of the bourgeois society may develop differently at different places, depending upon the local social and historical conditions. This variety of conditions may lead on to the achievement of political power by the working class through divergent ways and means. Peaceful struggle, waged through bourgeois political institutions, could be one of these and may prove, at times, quicker and more effective than a violent struggle. Marx, thus, has not ruled out the possibility of a peaceful transfer of power from the bourgeoisie to the working class.

Fundamental Break

We should note, however, that Marx has not made so far a definitive statement that the working class *will* be able to conquer political power and effect the socialist transformation in a given historical situation entirely through peaceful means. He seems reluctant to make this commitment. What can be the reason for this reluctance? A clue may be found in the following statements of Marx made, again, in September 1872:

> An historical development can remain 'peaceful' only so long as no forcible hindrances are placed in its path by those holding power in society at the time...the peaceful movement could become a 'violent' one on encountering the resistance of those interested in the old state of affairs...[26]

> ... the 'peaceful' development could quickly change into a 'violent' one through a rebellion by those with a stake in the old order...[27]

In other words, Marx feared that even where a peaceful change was possible, the bourgeoisie might resort to force to crush the peaceful ascent to power by the workers or their efforts to peacefully transform the structures of society after coming into power. This use of force by the bourgeoisie may compel the workers to become violent. We can see that even though Marx believed in the possibility of a peaceful change under certain socio-historical conditions, yet he thought that this possibility may not always be realised given the tendency on the part of the ruling classes to use all means to protect their interests. Engels supplemened this view of Marx in 1886 in his preface to the English edition of *Capital.* Talking of what Marx had said about England, he wrote: "He certainly never forgot to add that he hardly expected the English ruling classes to submit without a 'pro-slavery rebellion' to this peaceful and legal revolution".[28]

From the above-quoted statement it appears that according to Engels Marx was almost certain that the bourgeoisie will make use of violence to stop the peaceful revolution by the workers. As is clear, Engels attributes to Marx a degree of certainty he really did not enjoy. This certainty, however, was a feature of both Lenin's and Mao's opinion, both of whom believed that the bourgeois parliamentary institutions could not become a vehicle for the peaceful transformation of society by the working class. Revolution in bourgeois-demoratic societies, according to Mao, will take the form of primarily a civil war which will be preceded by a "long legal struggle...utilising parliament...organising trade unions and educating the workers".[29] These structures, in other words, served the purpose only of preparing the workers for the impending violent struggle. According to Lenin, similarly, "parliamentarism" was nothing more than "one of the means of enlightening and educating the proletariat and organising it in an independent class party". Therefore, it had "limited" historical importance. Lenin, in fact, went further and labelled parliamentarism as "an instrument of bourgeois oppression".[30]

So far as the existence of these institutions in England and America was concerned, Lenin was of the opinion that a peaceful change there through these institutions was perhaps possible in 1871 "when Britain was still...without a militarist clique and, to a considerable degree, without a bureaucracy"; in 1917, however, "at the time of the first great imperialist war", the alternative view held by Marx and Engels was "no longer valid", because at this moment both Britain and America, "the biggest and the last representatives...of Anglo-Saxon 'liberty', had "completely sunk" into the "morass of bureaucratic-military institutions which subordinate everything to themselves, and suppress everything".[31]

At first glance, Lenin seems to be only updating Marx and Engels. This, however, is not the only significance of these remarks. What looks like his refusal to equate the Britain of 1917 with that of 1871 is, in fact, his assertion that there is a need to make a violent revolution even in societies which Marx had accepted as democratic, and where a peaceful transformation was, therefore, possible. For, in spite of Lenin's argument to the contrary, the Britain of 1871 was not without its military and bureaucracy, nor had the Britain of 1917 fundamentally departed from democratic values and traditions. Although till 1917, when Lenin expressed the above opinion in *The State and Revolution*, he had many a time asserted that the bourgeoisie could not be overthrown without the use of violence, he had always done this, as we shall see later, in the context of Russia which at no time had a fully democratic system. By making the same assertion with regard especially to Britain, he effected a fundamental break with the position of Marx and Engels.

This conclusion gets confirmed when in the same book we see Lenin selectively quoting Engels to prove that universal suffrage was nothing more than "an instrument of bourgeois rule". Engels says in this quotation that universal suffrage is "the gauge of maturity of the working class. It cannot and will never be anything more in the present-day state". Lenin himself admits that Engels was referring here to the specific experience of the nineteenth century German social demoracy, but, forgetting this, he goes on to apply this experience sweepingly to the whole of contemporary Europe and condemns indiscriminately the Socialist Revolutionaries and Mensheviks, and the "opportunists of Western Europe", for expecting "just this 'more' from universal suffrage".[32]

Summing up, we may say that as per the alternate view of Marx and Engels a peaceful transformation of the bourgeois society was possible at places where democratic institutions, values and traditions had emerged and become entrenched. At such places, the proletariat could use these very institutions and effect the socialist change. They nevertheless made it clear that a violent revolution may become inevitable and necessary even at such places because the ruling classes may ultimately decide not to give up their power without an armed resistance. As for Lenin and Mao, neither of them subscribes to this changed position of Marx and Engels. According to them, bourgeois-democratic institutions may delay the onset of violence but they will not prevent its occurrence. They seem to be sure that the bourgeoisie will finally use force to crush even the peaceful movement of the workers. Such institutions, therefore, can be used only to organise and educate the working class for the coming violent revolution during the temporary phase of the peaceful, parliamentary struggle.

Lenin, in fact, seems to be extremely wary of these institutions. As is clear from his statements, he sees these institutions as nothing more than the instruments of perpetuating bourgeois rule. This position of Lenin cannot but be interpreted as the necessity of violent revolution in the bourgeois-democratic societies. It needs to be emphasised that, for Lenin, this necessity arises not in spite of but rather because of the presence of the bourgeois-democratic institutions.

NOTES

[1] Marx and Engels, *The German Ideology*, Progress Publishers, Moscow, 1976, p. 60.

[2] Marx, *The Poverty of Philosophy*, Progress Publishers, Moscow, 1975, p. 161. See also, Note 54, ibid., p. 214.

[3] Marx and Engels, *The Holy Family*, Progress Publishers, Moscow, 1975, p. 44.

[4] Ibid., pp. 43-44.

[5] Ibid., p. 43.

[6] Ibid., p. 44.

[7] Ibid., p. 43.

[8] Marx and Engels, "Manifesto of the Communist Party", *Selected Works*, Volume One, Progress Publishers, Moscow, 1976, p. 110.

[9] Ibid., p. 116.

[10] Ibid., p. 117.

[11] Ibid., p. 119.

[12] Ibid., p. 118.

[13] Lenin, "Two Tactics of Social Democracy in the Democratic Revolution", *Collected Works*, Volume 9, Foreign Languages Publishing House, Moscow, 1962, p. 30.

[14] Lenin, "A Retrograde Trend in Russian Social-Democracy", *Collected Works*, Volume 4, Foreign Languages Publishing House, Moscow, 1960, p. 276.

[15] See, *The Political Thought of Mao Tse-tung*, ed. Stuart R. Schram, Penguin Books, Harmondsworth, 1969, p. 296; and Jerome Ch'en, *Mao and the Chinese Revolution*, Oxford University Press, London, 1967, p. 71.

[16] Mao, in Schram, ibid., pp. 296-97.

[17] Mao, "Be Activists in Promoting the Revolution", *Selected Works of Mao Tse-tung*, Volume V, Foreign Languages Press, Peking, 1977, p. 495.

[18] Mao, "Problems of War and Strategy", *Selected Works*, Volume II, Foreign Languages Press, Peking, 1977, pp. 219 and 224-25.

[19] In the first volume of *Capital*, for example, Marx concluded that force was "the midwife of every old society pregnant with a new one". He had reached this conclusion on the basis of a detailed examination of the working of the different modes of production. Talking specifically of the bourgeois mode of production, he wrote : "Centralisation of the means of production and socialisation of labour at last reach a point where they become incompatible with their capitalist integument. This integument is burst asunder. The knell of private property sounds. The expropriators are expropriated". (See Marx, *Capital*, Volume 1, Progress Publishers, Moscow, 1977, pp. 703 and 715).

[20] Engels, "Principles of Communism", in Marx and Engels, *Selected Works*, Volume One, op. cit., p. 89.

[21] Engels, "Speeches in Elberfeld', the speech of February 15, 1845, in Marx and Engels, *Collected Works*, Volume 4, Progress Publishers, Moscow, 1975, p. 262.

[22] Quoted in Shlomo Avineri, *The Social and Political Thought of Karl Marx*, S. Chand and Company, New Delhi, 1977, p. 214. All emphases, unless otherwise stated, are in the original.

[23] Marx, quoted in David McLellan, *Karl Marx: His Life and Thought*, The Macmillan Press, London, 1973, p. 406.

[24] Marx, "The Civil War in France", in Marx and Engels, *Selected Works*, Volume Two, Progress Publishers, Moscow, 1976, p. 200.

[25] Marx, quoted in Avineri, , op. cit., pp. 215-16.

[26] Marx, "The Debate in the Reichstag on the Law Against Socialists", in Marx and Engels, *The Socialist Revolution*, Progress Publishers, Moscow, 1978, pp. 241-42.

[27] Marx, quoted by Monty Johnston, "Marx, Blanqui and Majority Rule", in Ralph Miliband and John Saville, eds., *The Socialist Register*, The Merlin Press, London, 1983, p. 312.

[28] Engels, Preface to the English edition of *Capital*, Volume I, op. cit., p. 703.

[29] Mao, "Problems of War and Strategy", *Selected Works*, Volume II, op. cit., pp. 219-22.

[30] Lenin, "The Social Democrats and Electoral Agreements", *Collected Works*, Volume 11, Foreign Languages Publishing House, Moscow, 1962, pp. 277-78.

[31] Lenin, "The State and Revolution", *Collected Works*, Volume 25, Progress Publishers, Moscow, 1964, pp. 415-16.

[32] Ibid., p. 393.

2

Inevitability of Violence: Underdeveloped Capitalism and the Absence of Bourgeois-democratic Institutions

As we know from the previous chapter, Marx and Engels believed that a violent socialist revolution was the inevitable end of bourgeois economic structures and their historical development. This was so because the political structures that logically followed from the exploitative economic structures were bound to be oppressive and authoritarian, leaving no room for peaceful revolutionary action on the part of the proletariat. Yet, on the other hand, they put forth the view that at places where bourgeois-democratic institutions have emerged and have become entrenched, the revolution could take a peaceful turn.

In the present chapter, we will find that although they themselves offer no such hint, Marx's and Engels' analysis of the political situation in the continental Europe as well as the conclusions they derive from it appear to follow from their alternate view mentioned above. The revolution in this part of Europe, they seem to argue, would assume a violent form because the bourgeois-democratic institutions either did not at all exist here, or, if they did exist in certain periods, they were in an extremely circumscribed form.

It could seem from the above that the violent or peaceful nature of the revolution, in the opinion of Marx and Engels thus understood, was now determined purely or at least primarily at the political level.

However, as our analysis of their position in this chapter will show, it seems to be their argument that the reason for the absence or circumscription of the bourgeois-democratic political institutions itself was the still underdeveloped state of the capitalist economic structures.

The reader might have noticed that this form of the argument imparts a totally new dimension to their position, namely that the bourgeois-democratic institutions are the essential political form of developed capitalism. This dimension could lead to the significant inference that Marx and Engels regarded a peaceful revolution as the more probable form of the socialist revolution in the developed capitalist societies. Needless to say, this would tantamount to a near reversal of their general position, elaborated at the beginning of Chapter 1, that in capitalist societies a violent socialist revolution was inevitable.

Apart from their role of ultimately determining the nature of the revolution, Marx and Engels attributed to economic structures another, secondary role: that of aiding the formation of potentially revolutionary situations by producing economic crisis and facilitating the working out of the most appropriate moment for attempting a revolution. All this could give the impression that their position remained totally structural-determinist. In actuality, however, we shall see that they introduced room for conscious subjective intervention. This intervention, nevertheless, must be based on an in-depth study of not only the prevailing economic conditions but also political circumstances, and should be made only at a moment when it is likely to yield maximum fruit.

Once again, it might seem that Marx and Engels should logically condemn attempts at intervention made at 'inappropriate' moments. But the picture is more complex. We shall see that, in practice, they refused to condemn such attempts once they had already been made.

They praised, even glorified, them saying that they had hastened the development of forces necessary for a successful revolution.

Before we elaborate this picture of Marx's and Engels' argument, we will point out and clarify an initial problem here. In this chapter, we are supposed to be analysing Marx's and Engels' views on the status of violence in the *socialist* revolution. However, in their writings to be explored here they do not make it sufficiently clear as to whether a socialist revolution begins only *after* the bourgeois revolution has completed its course. On the contrary, their own analysis of the bourgeois revolutions of the period in which the working class too participated leads one to conclude that they treated these revolutions as a kind of proto-socialist revolutions, so to speak. In any case, one does not come across in this analysis that abstract model of the revolutionary development, found in *The Communist Manifesto* for example, in which the bourgeois and the socialist revolutions form two successive stages. The model that emerges in this analysis is much more complex, so that it is difficult to see the two kinds of revolution as totally distinct from each other. Secondly, if one were to consider a socialist revolution to be one in which the working class fights *exclusively* against *only* the bourgeoisie, then out of the entire spectrum of the revolutions on the continental Europe beginning with the year 1848, the June revolution of 1848 in Paris and the March revolution of 1871, which culminated in the Paris Commune, would be the only ones left regarding which the view of Marx and Engels could be studied. But if one were to focus only on these two revolutions, one would have to leave out most of their views on the question of violence, for, as indicated earlier, a substantial portion of these views evolved during their discusison of the so-called bourgeois revolutions that took place during that period. We, therefore, do not propose to follow this approach.

We begin our discussion with the revolution of 1848-49, and with France.

Bourgeoisie and the State

Marx carried out his analysis of the political and, to some extent, the economic conditions in France both before and during the revolutions of 1848-49 primarily in the pamphlet *The Class Struggles in France: 1848 to 1850*, but also in *The Eighteenth Brumaire of Louis Bonaparte*, both written after the revolutionary wave had subsided. The first major flare up of the revolution had taken place on February 24, 1848 when the constitutional monarchy of Louis Philippe was overthrown.[1]

Attempting to characterise the nature of the economy during the reign of Louis Philippe, Marx described it as capitalism still in the making. "The struggle against capital in its highly developed modern form—at its crucial point, the struggle of the industrial wage-labourer against the industrial bourgeois—is in France a partial phenomenon".[2] Consequently, the state in France at the time was essentially the rule of the financial aristocracy. "Under Louis Philippe it was not the French bourgeoisie as a whole which ruled but only one fraction of it—bankers, stock market barons, railway barons, owners of coal and iron mines and forests, a section of landed proprietors who had joined their ranks—the so-called *financial aristocracy*". The industrial bourgeoisie, according to Marx, formed part of the "official opposition", and its opposition became increasingly strident as the "autocracy" of the financial aristocracy became "more absolute". As for the other classes, that is, the petty-bourgeoisie, the peasantry and the working class, they were "completely excluded from political power". The monarchy, which had very little political power in its own hands, was in continuous financial difficulties and was dependent in this matter upon the financial aristocracy. The financial aristocracy managed the economy in such a manner that while the other classes, including the industrial bourgeoisie, stagnated, the financial aristocracy itself kept increasing its wealth. Thus the rule of the financial aristocracy, in the words of Marx, "was nothing more than a joint-stock company for the exploitation of France's national wealth..." Under these conditions, the interests of the industrial bourgeoisie were "in permanent peril and at a permanent disadvantage..." The potato blight and the crop failure of 1845-46, the resulting rise in prices and the continent-wide commercial and industrial crisis of the period aggravated the discontent of the classes outside the political frame, which led to bloody conflicts at many places and finally to the February (1948) uprising in Paris under the leadership of industrial bourgeoisie.[3]

Marx nowhere explicitly says so, but it appears from the tone of his argument that he approved of the violent February upheaval under the conditions of which it was an inevitable product. These conditions were the total exclusion from the political power of all classes except the monarchy and the financial aristocracy, and the arbitrary economic management by the latter. The February revolution, however, was not strictly a proletarian revolution; it was essentially a bourgeois revolution, even though, along with the monarchy, a section of the bourgeoisie itself was its target. As Marx himself said, the revolution had only completed the rule of the bourgeoisie "by allowing all the property-owning classes to enter the political arena along with the financial aristocracy". The proletariat, nevertheless, had played an important role in the revolution, and it had played this role not for the sake of the bourgeoisie but for its own sake. In the words of Marx, "The workers had carried out the February revolution together with the bourgeoisie and they tried to secure their interests alongside the bourgeoisie..."[4] With the result that the workers gave a definite proletarian direction to the revolution. To quote Marx again: "Just as the workers in July days[5] had fought for and won the *bourgeois monarchy*, so in February days they fought for and won the bourgeois republic. Just as the July monarchy was forced to proclaim itself a *monarchy surrounded by republican institutions*, so the February republic was forced to proclaim itself a *republic surrounded by social institutions*. The proletariat forced this concession to be made too".[6]

Marx was aware, however, of the limited 'social' character of the revolution, and he attributed this limitation to the limited leverage that the proletariat had under the existing material conditions. As he put it: "In general, the development of the industrial proletariat is conditioned by the development of the industrial bourgeoisie…It is only the rule of the bourgeoisie which serves to tear up the material roots of feudal society and level that ground, thus creating the only possible conditions for a proletarian revolution". It was because of this reason that the French workers did not assert their interests "as the revolutionary interests of society itself, and…lowered the red flag before the tri-colour".[7]

In other words, in a situation where the bourgeois revolution has not yet been completed and as a consequence the proletariat has not been pushed forward to *lead* the historical movement, and, moreover, where the bourgeoisie, or a section of it, is willing to play its historical role, the proletariat should ally with the bourgeoisie, or with the leading section of it, and support its revolutionary actions, no matter what their nautre, violent or peaceful. As should be clear, the February revolution presents an instance of the situation where the proletariat supports a faction of the bourgeoisie in a violent movement.

A contrast was presented by the situation in Germany where, before the March (1848) revolution, the bourgeoisie, instead of waging a militant struggle against the absolutist monarchy, wanted a peaceful accommodation with it. Marx exhorted the workers in this situation to carry on, to the extent possible, peaceful political activity till the bourgeoisie had acquired the courage to fight against the monarchy.

The German economy, as per Marx's analysis, had already become before the March revolution essentially a bourgeois economy, whereas the state structure that was still continuing over this economy was monarchical, feudal and absolutist. The growth of industry, trade and modern agriculture had not only given birth to a new, bourgeois, class, it had also "fundamentally bourgeoisiefied" the nobility itself. The composite bourgeoisie that had thus emerged effectively controlled the economy without having as yet become able to lay its hands upon state power. The historical development, thus, had "conjured away" from under the feet of the monarchical, absolutist state the old economic foundation, and this form of state was now only "a fetter and a hindrance for the new...society with its changed... needs". Under these conditions, the bourgeoisie had to "lay claim to a share in political power, if only to assert its purely material interests...it had to assert its control of the resources of the state...which it considered to be its own creation". It had to "conquer a political position commensurate with its social position"[8] However, unlike the bourgeoisie of England and France in 1648 and 1789 respectively, the bourgeoisie of Germany wanted to achieve its aim without revolution due to an important reason. Whereas before the English and French revolutions the proletariat and the other non-bourgeois sections of the urban population had not as yet fully developed their own class interests separate from the interests of the bourgeoisie and, therefore, were not in a position to effectively challenge the would be power of the bourgeoisie by converting the bourgeois revolution into a revolution of the lower classes, this was not the case in Germany. "The German bourgeoisie had developed so sluggishly, so pusillanimously and so slowly, that it saw itself threateningly confronted by the proletariat in interests and ideas, at the very moment of its own threatening confrontation with feudalism and absolutism".[9] It therefore wanted "a peaceful transaction with the Crown..."[10] Hence its efforts to acquire the right of freedom of discussion and of free association within the overall framework of monarchy.[11]

It was in these conditions that immediately after the February revolution in France Marx opposed a plan for attempting an armed installation of a republican government in Germany. This plan was made by the German expatriate workers in Paris who had formed an armed body, called the German Legion, for this purpose.[12]

Marx's argument was that the conditions were not yet ripe for an armed attempt in Germany. In the words of Sebastian Seiler, a member of the Communist League, "Marx...developed the theme that February revolution should be viewed only as a superficial beginning of the European movement",[13] meaning that an armed insurrection in Germany at this moment would be premature. He suggested instead that they should go into Germany, singly or in small groups, and carry out propaganda work in order to strengthen the bourgeois movement there. And this is in fact what Marx, Engels and some other members of the League ultimately did. The Legion, however, persisted in its task and was badly defeated.[14]

Clearly, Marx was not sure of the success of an armed attempt by the workers from abroad at establishing a bourgeois-republican government in Germany when both the bourgeois and the non-bourgeois urban classes within Germany were not willing or ready to go in for such an attempt, even though the changes in the economy had prepared the ground for a bourgeois political revolution.

However, the failed revolution in Germany only a few days later showed that at least the non-bourgeois urban classes had been willing to attempt a violent insurrection and that Marx's assessment of *their* mood was in any case wrong. But the failure of the revolution and the non-participation of the bourgeoisie, on the other hand, proved that Marx had been right so far as the prospects of such a venture were concerned.

Conflicts within the Bourgeoisie

The character of the states that emerged in France and Germany after the February and March revolutions, respectively, continued to differ. So did the political behaviour of the bourgeoisie in the two states and so, also, the response of the workers, and of Marx, so far as the use of violent or peaceful methods was concerned.

The provisional republican government that was formed in France after the February revolution reflected the interests of all those classes that had participated in the revolution. The industrial bourgeoisie, the petty-bourgeoisie and the working class, all found a place in it.[15] But it was dominated by the representatives of the bourgeoisie,[16] and the political behaviour of the regime in the subsequent months revealed its true character.

In the words of Marx, "...the February republic was in reality—and could be nothing else but—a *bourgeois* republic, but the provisional government was forced by direct pressure of the proletariat to proclaim it a *republic with social institutions*...The promises made to the proletariat came to represent an intolerable danger for the new republic, and the provisional government's entire existence took the form of a struggle against the demands of the proletariat". In its milder form, this struggle revealed itself in such acts as the exclusion by the National Assembly of the representatives of the proletariat from the executive commission, and its rejection of the suggestion of a special ministry of labour. And it manifested its harsher form in decrees such as that of June 21, which ordered the forcible expulsion of all unmarried workers from the National Workshops, or their enrolment in the army. The result was the June 22 revolt by the workers which lasted for five days, was ruthlessly crushed, and in which thousands of workers were killed.[17]

The June revolt which, in the opinion of Marx, was "the first great battle...between the two great classes which divide modern society"[18] was characterised by him as "forced", "bold and revolutionary". "The Paris proletariat was forced into the June insurrection...", he wrote. But ultimately, it turned out to be for the good of the proletariat and its movement. "By making its burial place the birthplace of the bourgeois republic, the proletariat forced this republic to appear in its pure form, as the state whose avowed purpose it is to perpetuate the rule of the capital and the slavery of labour". On the other hand, its defeat convinced the proletariat of "the truth that the smallest improvement in its position remains a utopia within the bourgeois republic, a utopia which becomes a crime as soon as it aspires to become reality".[19] As Marx had written in an article in the *Neue Rheinische Zeitung* on June 29, that is, immediately after the revolt: "The momentary triumph of brute force has been purchased with the destruction of all the delusions and illusions of the February revolution...and the division of the French nation into two nations, the nation of owners and the nation of workers..."[20] Summing up his survey of the entire revolutionary movement in France during the years 1848-49 in *The Class Struggles in France*, he similarly wrote:

> What succumbed in these defeats was not the revolution. It was the pre-revolutionary traditional appendages, results of

> social relationships which had not yet come to the point of sharp class antagonism —persons, illusions, conceptions, projects from which the revolutionary party before the February Revolution was not free, from which it could be freed not by the victory of the February, but only a series of defeats.
>
> In a word, the revolution made progress, forged ahead, not by its immediate tragi-comic achievements, but on the contrary by the creation of a powerful, united counter-revolution, by the creation of an opponent in combat with whom only the party of the overthrow ripened into a really revolutionary party.[21]

We can see that Marx does not condemn the uprising, but he makes it clear that the conditions were not yet ripe for the success of the uprising. That was the reason for its immediate defeat. But the defeat is not ultimately regarded by him as a defeat but a victory, because the uprising and its suppression have aided and hastened the historical forces working towards a successful future proletarian revolution. It has crystallised the situation by making the workers realise the real intentions of their enemy, the bourgeoisie, which would not hesitate to use brute force to crush them when its interests so demanded:

> Only after being dipped in the blood of the *June Insurgents* did the tricolour become the flag of the European revolution—the red flag!
>
> And we exclaim: the revolution is dead!—Long Live the revolution![22]

Tactically also the revolt proved beneficial to the proletariat. By temporarily removing the proletariat from the stage and by putting an official stamp on the dictatorship of the bourgeoisie, the revolt made it obligatory for the middle classes—the petty-bourgeoisie and the peasantry—"to ally themselves with the proletariat, as their own situation became more intolerable and their antagonism to the bourgeoisie sharper."[23]

As for the bourgeoisie itself, after the suppression of the June insurrection the conflicts within itself began to come to the fore. The June suppression had been led by the republican faction of the bourgeoisie. But the republicans had relied heavily on the conservative sections of the bourgeoisie which were greater in number and which had previously ruled the state along with the monarchy and the feudals. Once peace was restored, these sections started asserting themselves with ever increasing vigour and slowly pushed the republicans out of power; the latter gave in tamely. The decline of republican bourgeoisie effectively started with the election of Louis Bonaparte, on December 10, 1848, as the president of France, and reached its apogee on December 2, 1851 when he brushed aside the republican constitution and declared himself the emperor.[24]

In Germany, although the March revolution had failed, one consequence of the revolution had been that the people were conceded limited democratic rights, and two legislative assemblies, the German National Assembly and the Prussian Assembly, to be indirectly elected, were promised.[25] The grant of limited constitutional rights strengthened the political power of the bourgeoisie but not in a manner which, according to Marx, the bourgeoisie would have preferred. It put the bourgeoisie in a difficult and uncomfortable position. Since its newly acquired power had been given to it as a consequence of a people's revolution, it had to represent, in the assemblies, the interests of these people too. But a fulfilment of these interests would have created a danger for its own interests. A further increase in people's power would have weakened the king whereas the bourgeoisie looked upon the king, who still held a monopoly over military and bureaucratic power, as its protector against the people. In the words of Marx: "If therefore the February revolution and its German after-effects were welcomed by the bourgeoisie because the direction of the state was thereby thrown into its hands, the revolution was also and just as much a disappointment, because it attached to bourgeois rule conditions the bourgeoisie was unwilling and unable to fulfil".[26]

So far as the monarchy was concerned, the March revolution, according to Marx, "by no means subjected the sovereign by the grace of God to the sovereign people. It only compelled the crown, the absolutist state, to come to terms with the bourgeoisie, to make an agreement with its old rival".[27]

So that the German state after the March revolution was a monarchical-bourgeois state, a state that was no longer absolutist but allowed limited constitutional rights to the people. And its was the existence of this latter fact that seems to have been crucial, for Marx, so far as the nature and direction of the proletarian politics in Germany during the period was concerned. This politics should be open and democratic, in accordance with the conditions brought into existence by the grant of constitutional freedoms, and it should aim at helping the ongoing bourgeois movement, howsoever timid and difficult, reach completion.

When Marx tried to put this politics into practice, he immediately came into conflict with the recognised leadership of the workers in Germany. The immediate issue was whether the workers' organisations should participate in the coming elections to the Prussian assembly and to the national parliament of Frankfurt. Andreas Gottschalk, a leader of the Cologne workers, the leading German industrial city, opposed the participation in elections. He believed that the elections would benefit the bourgeois republicans and not the workers as the workers' movement was not sufficiently strong to extract gains for itself through elections. He favoured an agitationist and confrontationist approach. Marx, on the other hand, was against keeping the workers isolated from the democratic political practice. He therefore helped to found a Democratic Society in Cologne which successfully sponsored a candidate for the Frankfurt parliament.[28] It was in pursuance of this policy of his again that in May 1848 Marx dissolved the Communist League in spite of the opposition of some members of the League.

According to Peter Roser, a member of the Cologne group of the League, "Marx considered the continuance of the League to be superfluous, since the aim of the League was not conspiracy but propaganda and under the present circumtances propaganda could be conducted openly and secrecy was not necessary since a free press and the right of association were guaranteed".[29] Marx himself said later that the League's activities "faded out of their own accord in that more effective means of carrying out our aims were available".[30] Even the policy of the paper *Neue Rhinische Zeitung* that Marx founded in Cologne during this period was consistent with his above-mentioned stand. The subtitle of the paper was "An Organ of Democracy", and its programme was limited to the demands of universal suffrage, direct elections and the abolition of all feudal dues and charges, etc. "The essence of the programme was", to quote McLellan, "the emancipation of the bourgeoisie with some concessions to workers and peasants."[31] In this context, Marx declared that "the proletariat has not the right to isolate itself—from its allies", meaning the radical wing of the bourgeoisie.[32]

However, Marx discontinued to advocae this policy in the subsequent months when the king started asserting his authority and there were clear indications that the bourgeoisie was giving in to him. The policy he now adopted was similar to the one he had asserted before the March revolution, namely, that a violent insurrection may ultimately become inevitable but the moment had not yet arrived for such an undertaking. In September (1848) there was an uprising in Frankfurt against the government over an armistice with Denmark. This led to the creation of an insurrectionary situation, a few days later, in Cologne when the population in general and the working class in particular wanted to have a clash with the government troops.[33] But the Democratic Society, being led, among others, by Marx and Engels, argued against an uprising just then. As Marx put it two weeks later (October 12, 1840):

> ...[T]he democrats told the workers...that under no circumstances did they want a putsch. At that moment, indeed, when there was no great question impelling the whole population to take part in the struggle, with the result that an uprising was bound to fail, such an action would be senseless, they said, and, still worse, would exhaust the workers before the day of decision, since tremendous events were expected in the next few days.[34]

It should be obvious that this shift in Marx's policy was caused by the change in the character of the German state which, while continuing to be a monarchical-bourgeois state in theory, had become in practice an absolute monarchy once again. This gets confirmed from Marx's appraisal of the role and status of the bourgeoisie in Germany in the immediately preceding months. In an article on November 6, 1848, he wrote:

> In Germany the bourgeoisie finds itself pressed into the retinue of absolute monarchy and feudalism before it has even made sure of the basic conditions for its own freedom and supremacy...[I]t plays the role of a slave, and makes the

> counter-revolution required by the despots who rule it...[I]t humbles itself in order to prevent the people from conquering. In the whole of history there is no more ignominious example of abjectness than that provided by the German bourgeoisie.[35]

This character and behaviour of the German bourgeoisie from March onwards convinced Marx that a pure bourgeois revolution, carried out by the bourgeoisie, was impossible in Germany. What was possible was either an absolutist, monarchical-feudal counter-revolution or a socialist-republican revolution made by the working class.[36]

In other words, by the end of 1848 Marx had given up his initial line that in Germany the working class must first help the bourgeoisie in carrying out bourgeois revolution before starting work exclusively for socialist revolution. Now the bourgeois and the socialist revolutions were to be coalesced into one, and this was to be done by the working class. This imperative had come about due to the abandonment by the bourgeoisie of its historical task, that of completing the bourgeois revolution, for the fear of an immediately following proletarian revolution. As we shall see below, according to Marx, such a revolution in an absolutist state maintained by the monarchical and feudal classes and acquiesced in or supported by the bourgeoisie had to be necessarily violent.

Shift in Stance

As is evident from the exposition above, Marx and Engels had nurtured the hope, till at least the middle of 1848, that the democratic bourgeoisie would create conditions conducive to the free development of the proletariat—conditions which would allow the workers to pursue their political interests peacefully. But the democratic bourgeoisie of France and Germany proved too weak, timid and opportunistic to fulfil their hope. It failed not only to protect and advance its own interests adquately, it even helped the old order to suppress the nascent proletarian movement wherever it felt threatened by its emergence. Marx and Engels, in their programme so far, had virtually ignored the working class leadership and organisations and had aligned themselves tactically with the radical democratic bourgeoisie. Their disillusionment with the latter now turned them towards the former.

They now entered a phase in which they abandoned their faith in peaceful political activity and vested it exclusively in revolutionary violence. Blaming the bourgeoisie for this radical turn in their attitude and politics, in November 1848 Marx wrote:

> The power of arms was defeated everywhere in the February and March days. Why? Because it represented nothing but the *governments*. After the June days the power of arms has conquered everywhere, because everywhere the *bourgeoisie* is to be found in collusion with the governments, while on the other side it has control of the official leadership of the revolutionary movement, and puts into operation all those half measures which have their natural outcome in an abortion.[37]

Marx argued, in this article, that if counter-revolution in Europe were to be allowed to run its natural course, it will meet its inevitable end on the shores of "the bankruptcy of the state", because an absolutist state will throttle the development of what was essentially a capitalist economy. However,

> ...the course of development will not wait for the payment-day of that promissory note drawn by the European states on European society. The devastating counter-blow to the June defeat will be struck in Paris. With the victory of the 'red

> republic' in Paris, the *armies* will be vomited forth from *inside* of the other countries and over the boundaries, and the *real power* of the contending parties will reveal itself in a pure form.[38]

Continuing in the same vein, Marx noted his indictment of the ruling classes and his hopes for violent counter-blow by the oppressed classes in the following words:

> The purposeless massacres perpetrated since the June and October events, the tedious offering of sacrifices since February and March, the very cannibalism of the counter-revolution, will convince the nations that there is only one means by which the murderous death agonies of the old society and the bloody birth throes of the new society can be shortened, simplified and concentrated—that is by revolutionary terror.[39]

As we know, Marx adopted this attitude at a moment in the history of the continental Europe when the bourgeois-democratic revolutions, in which the working class too had participated, failed to entrench the democratic bourgeoisie in power and establish bourgeois-democratic regimes. As things turned out, whereas in France it was the non-democratic sections of the bourgeoisie which emerged as the dominant partner in the regime, in Germany they retained a major say in decision-making despite the overall hegemony of the monarchy. As at both these places the democratic bourgeoisie had to share whatever little influence it had with the classes/groups which still owed allegiance to the pre-revolutionary regimes, the character of the new regimes remained largely authoritarian. Coupled with the fact that the defeated democratic bourgeoisie not only remained passive but also anti-working class, it was this character of these regimes that prompted Marx to adopt a stance that at the moment saw no alternative to a violent working class movement.

We should recall at this point that according to Marx the character of the economy primarily of Germany but also that of France to some extent had already become, before the revolutions, predominantly capitalist. It would not be wrong to infer from this that it was because of this shift in the character of the economies that Marx had been expecting the democratic bourgeoisie to take over the reigns of state power through these revolutions, something that the democratic bourgeoisie failed to do. So that a situation had been created where while the character of the economy was predominantly capitalist, the character of the state was still semi-feudal, semi-monarchical and only partly bourgeois—and hence, non-democratic. As we have said before, it is this non-democratic character of the state which appears to make, for Marx, a violent revolution inevitable.

The Authoritarian State

We have seen that for Marx it was the authoritarian character of the state that seemed the immediate determining factor behind a violent socialist revolution. This character of the state, however, was not very helpful in pinpointing the actual time when the revolution was likely to occur. For Marx, this task was facilitated much more by the state of the economy—that is, whether in a given period the economy of an authoritarian state was in an ascendant phase or was in deep crisis. Therefore, in addition to finding out the political conditons that were responsbile for the revolutions of 1848-49, Marx had also been concerned to know the economic conditions that had been instrumental in giving rise to the revolutions just then. His aim was also to compare these conditions with the conditions that prevailed immediately after the revolutions so that it could be precisely determined whether a revolution was likely to occur in the foreseeable future. In the event this likelihood was there, the policies and practices of the movement could be accordingly adjusted.

Marx's studies, which he conducted between June and September 1850, revealed that the revolutions were preceded by a severe economic crisis in all of Europe except the far eastern region. However, no such conditons were currently visible. Marx accordingly prophesied that the coming period would not be conducive to revolutionary upsurge.

According to Marx, the years 1837-42 had been the years of an almost uniterrupted depression. This was followed by a brief industrial and commercial prosperity in 1843-45. This prosperity gave birth simultaneously to overproduction and excessive speculation. The result of these two developments was the large-scale bankruptcies of the post-1845 years which continued up to the outbreak of the revolution. This was accompanied by the potato blight and a huge loss in corn harvest, which caused a steep rise in the corn prices in all European markets. During this entire period, the whole credit system collapsed and financial market was totally destroyed.[40]

The recovery from the crisis began in England, which had suffered the least from both the crisis and the revolutions, and was followed soon by that on the continent. The recovery was not, according to Marx, the result of counter-revolutionary stability and order, but of the renewed prosperity in England and the increased demand for industrial goods in the American and tropical markets. Marx summed up his conclusion of this survey in the following words:

> While this general prosperity lasts, enabling the productive forces of bourgeois society to develop to the full extent possible within the bourgeois system, there can be no question

> of a real revolution. Such a revolution is possible only at a time when *two factors* come into *conflict*: the *modern productive forces and the bourgeois forms of production*...A new revolution is possible only as a result of a new crisis...[41]

The Blanquist elements in the Communist League, particularly August Willich and Karl Schapper, did not agree with this analysis of Marx. They believed that it was possible to force a revolutionary uprising in Germany in any case. All that was needed, they argued, was a few daring individuals, and weapons.[42] They accused Marx of being a reactionary.[43] The conflict came to a head on September 15, 1850. In a meeting of the central committee of the League, Marx lashed out at his opponents as follows:

> Instead of the materialistic veiw of the *Manifesto* they bring forth the idealist one. Instead of the real conditions they point to the will as the major factor in revolution.
>
> While we tell the workers: "You have to endure and go through 15, 20, 50 years of civil war in order to change the circumctances, in order to make yourselves fit for power"—instead of that, you say, "We must come to power immediately..."[44]

Obviously, for Marx the material conditions enjoyed a primacy over the idealistic ones so far as the possibiity of a revolution and the determination of an appropriate time for it were concerned. As we know, Marx believed that the two factors that were most important in this context were an authoritarian state and an economy in crisis. We saw in this section that according to Marx the second of these factors was not present on the continental Europe during the period under focus. It was because of the absence of this factor in Europe just then that an attempt at insurrection would have been an exercise in foolhardiness. But what if both these factors were present? That is, what if the state were authoritarian and the economy passing through a crisis? Could, and should, an insurrection be attempted in such a situation? In other words, were both these conditions sufficient to create a situation in which a violent revolution could be attempted?

As we shall see below, Marx never formulated this question in this manner. But he answered it all the same through his pronouncements and his political behaviour during the subsequent years. However, in the process he also made a significant addition to his earlier views. This addition inhered in the realisation and its textual and practical expression that in addition to an authoritarian state and economic crisis, the presence of revolutionary consciousness in the proletariat was also necessary for constituting a revolutionary situation. Implied in this position was the assertion, first, that when both the other factors are present but the revolutionary consciousness in the proletariat is missing, one should not indulge in insurrectionary politics, and, second, that revolutionary consciousness in the proletariat need not necessarily follow from the other two factors, in any case, not immediately.

Marx adopted this position when the economic crisis that he had predicted, and had been waiting for, did not develop into an immediate proletarian revolution, although it stirred up the by now almost dormant labour movement in Europe and reawakened the old socialist groups of various hues. Marx and Engels played very little active role in the formation of the First International in 1864, the culmination of this fresh awakening of the European working class movement, but Marx was elected a member of the committee that was to draw up the rules of the International. The committee accepted, with small modifications, Marx's draft for the *Inaugural Address of the International.*[45]

As compared to his earlier writings, the *Inaugural Address* was mild both in tone and content. It did not give the workers any call for immediate revolutionary action. Marx seemed more concerned at this moment about the preservation of the unity of the international working class movement. It appears that he did not want to frighten away those elements in it which were hostile to the social revolution of the Marxian variety. Secondly, although the labour movement had grown over the years, yet the class consciousness of the workers and their leaders was not as sharp now as during the late forties. Pointing out these limitations, and talking in the context of the *Inaugural Address*, Marx wrote to Engels: "It was very difficult to frame the thing so that our view should appear in a form acceptable from the present standpoint of the workers' movement…It will take time before the reawakened movement allows the old boldness of speech".[46]

Minority Revolution

It may seem from the above that by 1864 Marx had abandoned or softened his previous militant approach to revolution on the continent. This, in any case, is the argument of George Lichtheim, according to whom the *Inaugural Address* was "the Charter of Social Democracy"[47] and the Marx of 1864 was "the theorist of labour movement…committed to democratic socialism".[48] Secondly, a corollary of our analysis in the pages immediately above should be that Marx and Engels would not advocate a violent struggle anywhere if the existing 'standpoint' of the workers' movement did not favour such a struggle. However, our analysis below will show that Marx and Engels not only continued to hold their pre-1864 approach to revolution on the continent, but also they severely criticised the workers' movement whenever and wherever it displayed any inclination to give up the militant road if the conditions, in their view, disfavoured such a step. They believed that the movement must either follow militant line or face condemnation. We will see that this was their attitude towards the German socialist movement. So far as the issue of their abadonment of the previous militant approach is concerned, they actually went, in the case of Russia, to the extent of hoping for a minority revolution at a place where the workers' movement had hardly begun.

The Paris Commune

We will begin by outlining their views on the upheaval that took place in Paris in 1871, and resulted in the Paris Commune (March 28, 1871—May 29, 1871). This development, in the opinion of Lichtheim, "did not permanently dislodge Marx from his mature standpoint",[49] but only "temporarily" influenced him to abandon "his realistic outlook of 1864..."[50]

The regime against which the workers revolted and established the Commune was no longer a monarchy but a bourgeois republic. The king had been defeated and captured by the Prussians in the immediately preceding Franko-Prussian war and a bourgeois-republican government had replaced him during the crisis.[51] However, according to Marx, this regime lacked a genuine bourgeois-democratic character. "[W]e hail the advent of the republic in France", he wrote, "but...that Republic has not subverted the throne, but only taken its place become vacant. It has been proclaimed, not as a social conquest, but as a national measure of defence". Further, according to him, "the stranglehold of the army and the police" remained under the control of those factions of the republican government which had been loyal to the monarch. Lastly, the republicans had "inherited from the Empire, not only ruins, but also its dread of the working class".[52] The implication of this characterisation of the French state at that moment was clear: the workers could not depend upon the institutions of this state to conquer power. In other words, an illegal, extra-institutional struggle was the only real option that they had. This comes out in the support Marx and Engels extended to the workers' revolt when it broke out on March 18.

However, they had believed before the revolt that the moment had not yet arrived for it. Marx had written in 1870, for example, that any attempt to overthrow the government "in the present crisis, when the enemy is almost knocking at the doors of Paris", would be "a desperate folly".[53] Engels had expressed a similar view when he wrote to Marx that the workers "would be needlessly crushed by the German armies and thrown back another 20 years".[54] When the revolt actually broke out, Marx considered it the result largely of an "accident". That accident was "the presence of Prussians in France and their position right before Paris". But Marx by no means denounced the revolt. "World history", he wrote to Ludwig Kugelmann, "would indeed be very easy to make if the struggle were taken up only on the condition that the prospects were unmistakably favourable",[55] meaning thereby that taking risk was, to a certain extent, natural, necessary and justified. We should recall that Marx had taken a similar position in 1850 in his *The Class Struggles in France*, and, before that, in 1848 when he had labelled the June uprising of Paris as premature and yet had praised it.

Marx's analysis of the tactics of the Commune also proves our point. Almost right from the beginnng he was pessimistic about the success of the Commune, but he blamed the Communards themselves for their impending failure. On April 7, 1871, he wrote to Wilhelm Leibknecht: "It seems the Parisians are succumbing. It is their own fault...a fault which was...due to their too great decency...they rather foolishly did not want to start a civil war". On April 12, he repeated these views in his letter to Kugelmann. "They ought to have marched at once on Versailles", he wrote, "They missed their opportunity because of moral scruples".[56]

Marx displayed, too, this militant attitude regarding the revolution on the continent in certain general remarks he made in the same period, remarks which sprang up during the course of his detailed appraisal of the functioning of the Commune. These remarks pertained to the strategy and tactics of the working class movement when the power has already been captured. He wrote: "The working class cannot simply lay hold of the readymade state machinery and wield it for its own purposes".[57] We get a clue to Marx's meaning when we read this remark in conjunction with what he had written to Kugelmann only a few days earlier. He had said: "If you look at the last chapter of my *Eighteenth Brumaire*, you will find that I declare: the next French Revolution will no longer attempt to transfer the bureaucratic-military apparatus from one hand to another, but to *smash* it, and this is the pre-condition for every real people's revolution on the continent."[58] We can see that Marx is advocating here the use of force after the political power proper has been seized in a revolution on the continent. In other words, he is advocating its use during the period of the reorganisation of the state.

Force may also have to be used to put down the bourgeois elements left over after the seizure of power, who may try to impede the work of the Commune. Such elements will still exist because the Commune does not do away with class struggles but only represents "the organised means of action" of the working class; it only begins the process leading towards the final emancipation of labour. Therefore, the commune may still have to undergo "catastrophe" in the form of "specific slave-holders' insurrections, which, while for a moment interrupting the work of peaceful progress, would only accelerate the movement by putting the sword into the hands of the Social Revolution".[59] A similar point was made by Engels in his article "On Authority", written between March 1872 and October 1873, in which he criticised the Bakuninists who opposed all authority. Talking of the nature of revolution, Engels said: "A revolution is... the act whereby one part of the population imposes its will upon the other part by means of rifles, bayonets and canon...And if the victorious party does not want to have fought in vain, it must maintain this rule by means of the terror which its arms inspire in the reactionaries". Giving the example of the Commune, Engels further said: "Would the Paris Commune have lasted a single day if it had not made use of this authority of the armed people against the bourgeois?" Engels, in fact, accused (like Marx had done before) the Commune of not having used this force "freely enough".[60]

Clearly, what Lichtheim calls Marx's "temporary abandonment" of his "realist outlook of 1864" was in fact a reassertion, under favourable conditions, of a belief he had never really given up, namely that in the continental Europe the revolution had to come through a violent struggle.

Germany

With regard to Germany, Marx and Engels severely criticised the reformist strategy and tactics of the German Social-Democratic Party (SPD) throughout the period from 1867 onwards when representative assemblies, elected through manhood suffrage, were again allowed there, but in such a manner that they had little control over the executive authority of the state, which remained in the hands of the king.[61] Thus, for example, condemning the Gotha Programme of 1875, on the basis of which the Social-Democratic Workers' Party (which later changed its name to the German Social-Democratic Party, mentioned earlier) had just been created, Marx wrote: "There is nothing in its political demands beyond the old and generally familiar democratic litany: universal suffrage, direct legislation...etc...which depend on the recognition of the so-called sovereignty of the people and are hence only appropriate in a *democratic republic*". He ridiculed the party for addressing such demands "which are only feasible in a democratic republic" "to a state which is no more than a military despotism and a police state, bureaucratically carpentered, embellished with parliamentary forms and disguised by an admixture of feudalism although under the influence of bourgeoisie, and then to assure this same state into the bargain that they imagine that they can impose these demands on it 'by legal means'". "Even vulgar democrats", continued Marx, "tower mountains above this kind of democratism which keeps within the bounds of what is allowed by the police and disallowed by logic".[62] Two year later, Engels made light of Eugen Duhring, a German philosopher and economist, in a similar fashion. Speaking of the role of force in revolution, he wrote: "It is only with sighs and groans that he admits the possibility that force will perhaps be necessary for the overthrow of an economic system of exploitation...And this in Germany, where a violent collision...may, after all, be forced on the people..."[63] Marx returned to this issue once again in 1880 when, in a letter to Henry M. Hyndman, he contrasted the situation in England with that in Germany and remarked that the "military despotism" in the latter made a "revolution" necessary.[64]

Since the SPD did not change its policies despite the fact that in 1878 Bismark had imposed the Anti-Socialist Law (the law was lifted only in 1890) which prohibited the formation or continuation of any organisation which openly preached socialism or communism,[65] Engels continued to criticise the party after the death of Marx. His critique of the Draft Democratic Programme of the party in 1891 was in the familiar vein. In his critique, he attacked the "opportunism" that was steadily "gaining ground in a large section of the Social-Democratic Press". He condemned these elements for believing that the "present legal order in Germany was adequate for putting through all party demands by peaceful means," without asking themselves whether in Germany they "will not have to smash the fetters of the still semi-absolutist, and moreover indescribably confused political order." He made it clear that it was only in democratic republics, or in monarchies where the democratic institutions had become entrenched and powerful, that it could be possible to bring communism in a peaceful manner. But in Germany, where it "was not permitted to advance even a republican party programme openly", the belief that a communist society could be established "in a cosy, peaceful way" was "totally mistaken".[66]

It only remains to quote Engels' remarks in his famous 1895 introduction to Marx's pamphlet *The Class Struggles in France* to show that his appraisal of the situation in Germany continued to be different from that of the SPD till the very end. It is revealing, in this context, that the more militant passages from this introduction were deleted by the cautious SPD leadership, and that Engels allowed it to be published in this edited form only under protest. "I am of the opinion", he had written while protesting, "that you gain nothing by preaching a complete abstinence from violence. No one believes it and no party in any country goes so far as to give up the right to withstand illegality arms in hand".[67]

In the introduction itself, Engels speaks of the post-1870 Germany after briefly reviewing the history of the workers' movement in Europe. He writes: "...here, too, the conditions of the struggle had essentially changed. Rebellion in the old style, street fighting with barricades which decided the issue everywhere up to 1848, was to a considerable extent obsolete". A few pages later, Engels writes these often-quoted sentences: "The time of surprised attacks, of revolutions carried through by small conscious minorities at the head of unconscious masses, is past. Where it is a question of a complete transformation of the social organisation, the masses themselves must also be in it, must themselves already have grasped what is at stake, what they are going in for, body and soul."[68]

At a superficial glance, it could look as if Engels were suggesting an abandonment of violent struggle. However, in our opinion he is speaking here purely from the military point of view. In the first quotation, he only says that "rebellion in the old style", that is, "street fighting with barricades", had become "considerably" obsolete. In other words, it is not rebellion that has become obsolete, but the old style of rebellion. And even the obsolescence of the old style is not total. In the second quotation, Engels says that the method of making revolution by small minorities through surprise attacks was now outdated. Now the masses "themselves" must be "in it", that is, in revolution. This becomes more clear when we read the following words of Engels: "Does that mean that in future street-fighting will not play any role? Certainly not. It only means that the conditions since 1848 have become far more unfavourable for civilian fighters and far more favourable for the military. In future, street-fighting can, therefore, be victorious only if this disadvantageous situation is compensated by other factors. Accordingly, it will occur more seldom in the beginning of a great revolution than its farther progress, and will have to be undertaken with greater forces".[69]

Russia

In Russia, too, Marx and Engels believed, a violent revolution remained the only way socialism could be reached. However, this revolution need not necessarily be made by the working class; it could be made, or at least led, by some revolutionary group on behalf of the village communes that had historically been a dominant feature of the Russian rural society and in the later half of the nineteenth century were still in existence, although they had now fallen on bad days. If the revolution took this latter course, the Russians could totally bypass the capitalist stage of development and land straight into socialism via regenerated village communes. Further, both Marx and Engels made it clear in their own separate ways that the revolution in Russia need not necessarily be a majority affair. It becomes clear from their statements in this connection that if the revolution actually assumed a minority form it would still meet their approval.

A detailed and exact characterisation of the Russian state and economy of the period is not available in Marx's and Engels' writings. But their pronouncements show that they were aware of the monarchical and despotic nature of the state and a mixed kind of agricultural economy in which, after the serfdom was abolished in 1861, village communes, big landlords, and middle and poor peasants all existed together.

Further, the writings at least of Marx give evidence of the fact that he felt it desirable that Russia *should* bypass the capitalist phase of development. Dissociating himself from those socialists who wanted Russia to rapidly develop into a capitalist society so that a socialist revolution of the traditional Marxian variety could be attempted, and condemning the newly-emerging capitalists who were bent upon destroying the village commune, Marx wrote in November 1877: "If Russia continues to pursue the path she has followed since 1861, she will lose the finest chance ever offered by history to a people and undergo all the fatal vicissitudes of the capitalist regimes".[70]

This jump to socialism via village commune could, however, be made, emphasised Marx, only through a revolution. In a draft of his letter to Vera Ivanovna Zasulich, in February-March 1881, he said: "In order to save the Russian commune there must be a Russian

Revolution. And the Russian government and the 'new pillars of society' are doing their best to prepare the masses for such a catastrophe. If the revolution takes place at the right time, if it concentrates all the forces to ensure the free development of the village commune, the latter will soon emerge as the regenerative force in Russian society and is something superior to those countries which are still enslaved by the capitalist regime".[71]

The people who, in addition to Marx, wanted to bring about this development were various populist groups which had become active after 1861 when some political activity was allowed in Russia. These groups believed that will played a catalytic role in revolution, meaning that a revolution could be created in rural Russia.[72] Marx particularly admired the group Narodnaya Volya and after the assassination of Alexander II praised the group as "brave people with no melodramatic poses, straightforward, realistic and heroic".[73] At the same time, he condemned such socialist exiles as George Plekhanov and P. Axelrod for not believing in "politico-revolutionary action". "In order to make propaganda in Russia", he sarcastically remarked, "these gentlemen…go away to Geneva!"[74]

Engels too was expecting an immediate revolution in Russia. And he was so eager to see this revolution that he was willing to accept it even if it were to be made by a small minority. In a letter to Vera Zasulich, on April 23, 1885, he wrote: "What I know…about the situation in Russia makes me think that the Russians are approaching their 1789. The revolution…*may* break out any day. In these circumstances the country is like a charged mine which only needs a match to be applied to". Further on in the same letter, Engels made these significant remarks: "This is one of the exceptional cases where it is possible for a handful of people to *make* a revolution, i.e., by giving a small impetus to cause a whole system, which…is in no more than labile equilibrium, to come crashing down…[I]f ever

Blanquism—the fantastic idea of overturning an entire society by the action of a small group of conspirators had a certain raison d'être, that is certainly so now in Petersburg".[75]

As should be clear, this was for the first time in their entire political career that Marx and Engels approved, in so many words, a minority revolution even before it had actually taken place. However, they adopted this position because in their perception, firstly, the old Russian system had become so weak and unstable that it would need no more than a handful of people to pull it down, and, secondly, even though the entire population may not be willing to participate in the revolution, a majority of it was uniformly hostile to the existing regime.

NOTES

[1] Franz Mehring, *Karl Marx: The Story of His Life*, George Allen and Unwin, London, 1948, p. 152; and David Riazanov, *Karl Marx and Friederich Engels: An Introduction to Their Lives and Work*, Monthly Review Press, New York and London, 1973, p. 85.

[2] Marx, "The Class Struggles in France: 1848 to 1850", in *Surveys from Exile: Political Writings*, Volume 2, ed. David Fernbach, Penguin Books, Harmondsworth, and New Left Review, London, 1973, p. 46.

[3] Ibid., pp. 36-41. Emphases, unless otherwise indicated, are in the original.

[4] Ibid., pp. 43 and 45.

[5] Marx has in mind the revolution of July 1830 in France.

[6] Marx, "The Class Struggles in France", in *Surveys from Exile: Political Writings*, Volume 2, op. cit., p. 44.

[7] Ibid., p. 46.

[8] Marx, "The Bourgeoisie and the Counter-Revolution", in *The Revolutions of 1848: Political Writings*, Volume 1, ed. David Fernbach, Penguin Books, Harmondsworth, and New Left Review, London, 1973, p. 189.

[9] Ibid., p. 193.

[10] Ibid., p. 191.

[11] Ibid., p. 190.

[12] David McLellan, *Karl Marx: His Life and Thought*, The Macmillan Press, London and Basingstoke, 1973, pp. 190-92; and Mehring, op. cit., p. 154.

[13] Quoted in McLellan, ibid., pp. 192-93.

[14] Riazanov, op. cit., p. 86.

[15] Marx, "The Eighteenth Brumaire of Louis Bonaparte", in *Surveys from Exile: Political Writings,* Volume 2, op. cit., p. 152.

[16] Marx, "The Class Struggles in France", in *Surveys from Exile*, ibid., p. 41.

[17] McLellan, op. cit., p. 202; and Marx, ibid., pp. 57-58.

[18] Marx, ibid., p. 58.

[19] Ibid., pp. 60-61.

[20] Marx, "The June Revolution", in Marx and Engels, *Collected Works*, Volume 7, Progress Publishers, Moscow, 1977, p. 144.

[21] Marx, "The Class Struggles in France: 1848 to 1850", Marx and Engels, *Selected Works*, Volume 1, Progress Publishers, Moscow, 1976, p. 205.

[22] Ibid., p. 227.

[23] Marx, "The Class Struggles in France", in *Surveys from Exile: Political Writings*, Volume 2, op. cit., p. 61.

[24] Ibid., pp. 62 and 67, footnote 61.

[25] McLellan, op. cit., p. 199; and Marx, in *The Revolutions of 1848: Political Writings,* Volume 1, op. cit., pp. 113 and 115, footnotes 3 and 7 respectively.

[26] Marx, "The Bourgeoisie and Counter-Revolution", in *The Revolutions of 1848*, ibid., p. 191.

[27] Ibid., p. 195.

[28] McLellan, op. cit., p. 196.

[29] Quoted in ibid., pp. 196-97.

[30] Quoted in ibid., p. 197.

[31] Ibid., p. 201.

[32] Quoted in ibid., p. 202.

[33] Ibid., pp. 206-08.

[34] Marx, "The Cologne Revolution", in *The Revolutions of 1848: Political Writings*, Volume 1, op. cit., p. 169.

[35] Marx, "The Victory of the Counter-Revolution in Vienna", in *The Revolutions of 1848*, ibid., p. 174.

[36] Marx, "The Bourgeoisie and the Counter-Revolution", in *The Revolutions of 1848*, ibid., p. 212. Marx wrote this on December 31, 1848. Earlier on December 5, the king had already dismissed the Prussian assembly and proclaimed his own constitution. See, ibid., p. 187, footnote 95.

[37] Marx, "The Victory of the Counter-Revolution in Vienna", in *The Revolutions of 1848*, ibid., p. 175.

[38] Ibid., p. 176.

[39] Marx, "The Victory of the Counter-Revolution in Vienna", in Marx and Engels, *Collected Works*, Volume 7, op. cit., pp. 505-06.

[40] Marx and Engels, "Review: May-October 1850", in *The Revolutions of 1848: Political Writings*, Volume 1, op. cit., pp. 284-91.

[41] Ibid., p. 303, footnote 47.

[42] Riazanov, op. cit., p. 101.

[43] McLellan, , op. cit., p. 247.

[44] Quoted in Shlomo Avineri, *The Social and Political Thought of Karl Marx*, S. Chand and Company, New Delhi, 1977, p. 195.

[45] Riazanov, op. cit., pp. 109, 129 and 137-55.

[46] Marx, in Marx and Engels, *Selected Correspondence*, Progress Publishers, Moscow, 1975, pp. 139-40.

[47] George Lichtheim, *Marxism: An Historical and Critical Study*, Routledge and Kegan Paul, London, 1974, p. 103.

[48] Ibid., p. 99.

[49] Ibid., p. 126.

[50] Ibid., p. 105.

[51] See David Fernbach's introduction to Marx, *The First International and After: Political Writings*, Volume, 3, ed. Fernbach, Penguin Books, Harmondsworth, and New Left Review, London, 1981, pp. 30-31.

[52] Marx, "Second Address of the General Council of the International Working Men's Association on the Franco-Prussian War", in Marx and Engels, *Selected Works*, Volume 2, Progress Publishers, Moscow, 1976, p. 200.

[53] Ibid.

[54] Engels, in Marx and Engels, *Selected Correspondence*, op. cit., p. 234.

[55] Marx, ibid., p. 248.

[56] Ibid., pp. 246-47.

[57] Marx, "The Civil War in France", in Marx and Engels, *Selected Works*, Volume 2, op. cit., p. 217.

[58] Marx, in Marx and Engels, *Selected Correspondence*, op. cit., p. 27.

[59] Marx, in *Karl Marx: Selected Writings*, ed. David McLellan, Oxford University Press, Oxford, 1977, pp. 556-57.

[60] Engels , in Marx and Engels, *Selected Works*, Volume 2, op. cit., p. 379.

[61] See G. D. H. Cole, *Socialist Thought: Marxism and Anarchism*, 1850-1890, Macmillan & Co. Ltd., London, 1954, pp. 241-42; and Fernbach's intruduction to Marx, *The First International and After: Political Writings*, Volume 3, op. cit., p. 53.

[62] Marx, "Critique of Gotha Programme", in *The First International and After: Political Writings*, Volume 3, ibid., pp. 355-56.

[63] Engels, *Anti-Duhring*, Progress Publishers, Moscow, 1975, p. 211.

[64] Marx, in Marx and Engels, *Selected Correspondence*, op. cit., p. 314.

[65] Cole, op. cit., p. 256; and Fernbach's introduction to Marx, *The First International and After: Political Writings*, Volume 3, op. cit., p. 62.

[66] Engels , "A Critique of the Draft Social-Democratic Programme of 1891", in Marx and Engels, *Selected Works*, Volume 3, Progress Publishers, Moscow, 1976, pp. 434-35.

[67] Engels, quoted in David McLellan, *Engels*, Fontana/Collins, Glasgow, 1977, p. 50.

[68] See Engels' introduction to Marx's "The Class Struggles in France: 1848-1850", in Marx and Engels, *Selected Works*, Volume 1, op. cit., pp. 196 and 199-200.

[69] Ibid., p. 199.

[70] Marx, "To the Editorial Board of the 'Otechestvenniye Zapiski' ", in Marx and Engels, *The Socialist Revolution*, Progress Publishers, Moscow, 1978, p. 238.

[71] Marx, "First Draft of the Reply to V. I. Zasulich's Letter", in Marx and Engels, *Selected Works*, Volume 3, op. cit., p. 161.

[72] McLellan, *Karl Marx: His Life and Thought*, op. cit., p. 439.

[73] Marx to Jeny Lougnet, quoted in McLellan, ibid., p. 441.

[74] Marx to F. Sorge, quoted in McLellan, ibid.

[75] Engels to Vera Ivanovna Zasulich, in Marx and Engels, *Selected Correspondence*, op. cit., p. 362.

3

Inevitability of Violence: Underdeveloped Capitalism and the Monarchical-feudal State

Our argument in Chapter 2 was as follows. Marx and Engels appeared to believe that the socialist revolution would assume a violent form in societies in which the bourgeoisie had become the predominant class in the economic sphere but where the bourgeois-democratic institutions were totally or partially absent or lacked entrenchment. In such societies, the monarchical and feudal classes would still control the political structures or retain enough power to effectively influence the policies of the state. This belief followed from their alternate view of the nature of the revolution in bourgeois societies. Implicit in this position, we said, was the argument that the absence or lack of entrenchment of the bourgeois-democratic institutions was itself due to inadequate development of capitalist economic structures. Inadequate development of these structures made it possible for the monarchical and feudal classes to retain total or partial hold over the state even where their economic base had largely eroded or had become historically obsolescent. This situation kept the state, as before, authoritarian.

Lenin is in conformity with Marx and Engels so far as the violent nature of the revolution in an authoritarian state is concerned. But he differs with them in that he does not attribute the authoritarian nature of the state only to the absence or lack of entrenchment of bourgeois-democratic institutions. We have seen in Chapter 1 that Lenin regards the bourgeois-democratic institutions themselves as authoritarian with respect to the subordinate classes. It should follow from Lenin's view, then, that a violent revolution is inevitable in an autocratic state. We shall see in the present chapter that with regard to tsarist Russia this exactly is the opinion of Lenin. However, by adopting this position about tsarist Russia Lenin wishes to assert that under autocratic political conditions a violent revolution is doubly inevitable. This inevitability, however, is a direct consequence of not only the autocratic nature of the political structures; it is also rooted in the economy which, in the case of Russia, has already become capitalist but in which the capitalist mode of development is still in the early stages of its growth, thus keeping the state predominantly monarchical-feudal and autocratic.

Lenin, however, does not confine himself to the analysis of the domestic structures and situation while attempting to determine the nature of socialist revolution in Russia. He extends his analysis beyond its borders and examines the determining impact of European conditons upon the nature of Russian revolution. We will find him arguing that in the period of imperialist war the socialist revolution cannot but be violent. The form that this revolution should take is that of civil war. This is so because during the imperialsit war the monarchical-feudal or even the bourgeois state becomes all the more autocratic and authoritarian.

In addition, our analysis will show that Lenin never proposed a violent insurrection in Russia until the conditions became largely conducive for such an attempt. In the initial years, when he had not yet reached any definite conclusion about the nature of these conditions, he refused to take a definite stand on the nature of revolution. It was only after he had become fully conversant with the conditions that he started insisting on the necessity of a violent revolution. Even then, he repeatedly stressed the need to exploit every opportunity to further the cause of revolution through peaceful means and to not go in for insurrection till the most opportune moment. His insistence on using the semi-parliamentary body, the Duma, for propaganda purposes throughout the period of its existence, and his refusal to make a violent bid for power when a majority of the workers were supporting the soviets after the March 1917 revolution, are two major instances of this attitude.

Our approach in this chapter will remain the same as in the previous one. We will explicate and discuss Lenin's views in their historical background. And we will start with Lenin's characterisation of the Russian economy and state. We will then trace the evolution of his views on the question of violence from 1897 to the end of 1905 when he finally realised that there was no alternative to violent revolution in the autocratic Russian conditions. However, even at this moment, Lenin's views were not fully formed. The reason was the absence of parliamentary institutions in Russia. It was only in the late 1905 that the first such institution, the Duma, came into being. Therefore, we will analyse next Lenin's views primarily in the context of Duma. In addition, his attitude towards the bourgeois-democratic regime that came into power after the March 1917 revolution will also be discussed. It is here that we will fully come to know his assessment of democratic institutions and their role in bringing about systemic change. Finally, we will elaborate Lenin's conception of a violent revolution in Russia in the backround of the period starting with the First World War.

The Russian Economy and State

Lenin believed that by the year 1890 the Russian economy had become a completely capitalist economy. He concluded this on the basis of an analysis of the nature of the production system not only in the industrial sphere but also in agriculture, the latter having been rapidly modified after the land reforms of 1861. His arrival at this understanding was gradual, beginning with the early 1890s and spanning a period of nearly ten years. On the other hand, the Russian state represented to Lenin the interests of both the monarchical-feudal and the bourgeois classes, and was autocratic in its nature. Obviously for Lenin, the character of the economy was not fully reflected in the political structures in which the elements representing the old feudal economy still dominated.

Attempting to explain "what shape the Russian economy was taking", Lenin wrote in 1893 that capitalism was "already the main background of the economic life of Russia". He said that "agricultural and peasant community" was "splitting into a bourgeoisie and a proletariat", and as a result "vast mass(es) of peasants" were "losing their economic independence".[1]

By next year, Lenin's understanding had become still more unambiguous. Making fun of Narodniks' analysis of the Russian economy, he stated that "the reality of our environment is capitalist economy".[2] He emphasised that because of the development of the "commodity economy" throughout Russia after the reforms of 1861 not only was the Russian bourgeoisie "already in control of the people's labour everywhere", but it was also bringing "pressure to bear upon the government, initiating, compelling and determining the bourgeois character of its policy..."[3]

Lenin developed these ideas further in the following years. Noting the "systematic, universal and regular" exploitation indulged in by the kulaks in rural Russia, he described it as a "manifestation of capitalism in agricultrue..." It was "the domination of capital in its primary forms, capital which, on the one hand, engenders the urban, banking...capitalism...and, on the other hand, is supported and fed by this capitalism...in a word...it is one of the aspects of the capitalist organisation of the Russian national economy".[4]

Such development of capitalism in rural Russia was not an "accident" but a "necessity". Once the peasant becomes a commodity producer (and all peasants in Russia, in Lenin's view, had already become so), conditions are created which lead to the concentration of wealth in the hands of a few while the masses are reduced to poverty and are forced to sell their labour. In Russia this had begun to happen right after the reforms of 1861 when landlords introduced machines and technical implements and started using hired labour on a large scale. Those who benefitted from these developments extended their tillage and improved their farms whereas the former tenants and smaller peasants were converted into proletariat.[5]

So far as the development of capitalism in industry was concerned, the process had gone even further and reached a higher level. Here too the procss had been affected by the emancipation of peasants in 1861. The emancipation had led to a complete change in the living conditions of the mass of people. Small artisans were destroyed by big factories which proliferated very rapidly. These factories also marginalised petty proprietors and turned most into wage workers. Similarly, marginalisation of peasants in villages initiated massive movement of rural population; those who could not find employment in capitalised agricultrual farms moved to towns and industries. Thus the small-scale producer in both towns and villages was being ruined, and small-scale production was being replaced by large-scale production in which the former small producers were "just hirelings employed for wages by the capitalist..."[6] This was accompanied by the replacement of "small financial resources in the hands of individual proprietor by enormous sums employed as capital", and of the "small, insignificant profits by profits running into millions". Thus the growth of capitalism "was leading everywhere to the growth of luxury and riches". These, however, were confined to the class of owners. So far as the workers were concerned, as the "capital grew bigger it increased its pressure" on them, "turning them into paupers; compelling them to devote all their time to factory", and forcing their wives and children to go to work.[7]

It was this increasingly capitalised economy that the Russian state represened, promoted and protected. It was difficult to discern this, however, without a close look. Russia's was an absolute and unlimited monarchy. The tsar alone promulgated laws, appointed officials and controlled them. For this reason, it seemed as though the tsar and the tsarist government were totally independent of all classes and accorded equal treatment to all. But in reality, all officials were chosen exclusively from the propertied classes and all of them were subject to the influence of big capitalists, who made the ministers "dance to their tune" and achieved whatever they wanted.[8]

As for the common people, not only the workers but also others were, according to Lenin, deprived of political rights. They had no influence in proposing and making new laws or repealing old ones. They had no control over officials and could not check their activities or demand their prosecution. They did not have the right to even discuss the affairs of the state let alone hold meetings or form unions or parties. The capitalists, on the other hand, not only influenced the policies of the state indirectly, they had also been provided with direct means of achieving this through associations, chambers of trade etc., all of which were recognised by the state.[9]

All this could give the impression that the autocracy fully identified with, and worked exclusively on behalf of, the bourgeois class. This, according to Lenin, was not true. The autocracy was independent of the bourgeoisie to a significant extent and its interests coincided with those of the latter only in certain respects and to a certain degree. For example, the autocracy gave the bourgeoisie a free hand in the matter of exploiting the workers, but at the same time it hindred, through many of its other policies, the development of modern productive forces from which the bourgeoisie stood to gain. Frequently, it happened that the interests of the autocracy coincided only with those of certain strata of the bourgeois class. It was in such circumstances that the interests of some other bourgeois strata gave rise to a liberal opposition to the autocracy.[10]

Relative independence of the autocracy, and only limited degree of congruence between the economic and political structures, could be explained, believed Lenin, by the fact that the spread of capital in Russia was still in its early stages and had not yet eliminated totally the remnants of the erstwhile feudal economy. "The capitalist basis of contemporary relations", he said, "should not hide the still powerful relics of the 'old-nobility' stratum which have not yet been destroyed by capitalism precisely because it is underdeveloped".[11] These relics of the pre-capitalist serf-owning social system, by retarding the "development of the productive forces in the highest degree", also rendered "impossible the complete and all-round development of the proletariat's class struggle". They were responsible for keeping the "entire people in a state of ignorance and subjection, denying them all rights". The tsarist autocracy was the "most outstanding of these remnants… and the most dangerous enemy of the proletarian emancipation movement…". For these reasons, it was necessary to adopt "the overthrow of the tsarist autocracy" as "the immediate political task" of the Russain Social Democratic Labour Party.[12]

It becomes clear from the above account that for Lenin low level of development of the capitalist economy in Russia was responsible for the pre-dominantly monarchical-feudal and, therefore, autocratic character of the Russian state. Thus, Lenin's identification of the autocracy as the main enemy of the working class and the removal of the autocracy as its immediate goal followed directly from this character of the Russian economy of that time. Clearly, his advocacy of violent methods of struggle in Russia was also its consequence.

Methods of Struggle

Lenin's realisation that violent methods of struggle were the only suitable ones in the Russian conditions, however, was arrived at only gradually. In the beginning he would not commit himself as to which means, violent or peaceful, were to be employed in the impending struggle against the Russian state. The reason was lack of adequate and certain knowledge of the conditions that existed in Russia at that moment and those that were likely to emerge in the near future. Nevertheless, his rejection of purely conspiratorial tactics and his preference for involving the broader masses of the proletariat in the movement were quite clear even at this stage.

The first definite statement that Lenin made about the methods of struggle was in his pamphlet *The Tasks of the Russian Social Democracy*, written at the end of 1897. Answering the criticism of Social-Democrats' methods of political struggle by P. L. Lavrov, a theoretician of the group Narodnaya Volya, Lenin made the following significant remarks:

> To discuss in advance what methods this organisation will resort to in order to deliver a smashing blow at the autocracy, whether, for instance, it will prefer insurrection, a mass political strike, or some other form of attack, to disuss these things in advance and to decide this question now would be empty doctrinairism...for the solution of the problem depends on

> the state of the working class movement, on its breadth...on the attitude of other social elements to the proletariat and to the autocracy, on the conditions governing home and foreign politics—in a word, it depends on a thousand and one things which cannot be guessed, and which it would be useless to try to guess in advance...[13]

In the same pamphlet Lenin had earlier condemned and ridiculed the Narodniks for their conspiratorial methods:

> To the Narodvoltsi, the term political struggle is synonymous with the term political conspiracy!...Blanquist, conspiratorial traditions are fearfully strong among the [Narodvoltsi], so much so that they cannot conceive of political struggle except in the form of political conspiracy. The Social-Democrats, however, are not guilty of such a narrow outlook; they do not believe in conspiracies; they think that the period of conspiracies has long passed away, that to reduce political struggle to conspiracy means, on the one hand, immensely restricting its scope, and, on the other hand, choosing the most unsuitable methods of struggle.[14]

A little later, Lenin had added: "...[T]he Russian Social-Democrats have never forgotten the political conditions here, they have never dreamed of being able to form a workers' party in Russia legally...But they have always thought and continue to think that...the fight against the autocracy must consist not in organising conspiracies, but in educating, disciplining and organising the proletariat, in political agitation among the workers...".[15]

Writing on the same issue two years later in 1899, Lenin admitted "the necessity of learning revolutionary techniques and secret organisation from the old Russian masters", but stressed on the "duty" of the Social-Democrats to assess them "critically" and build their "own" organisation "independently". Continuing his attack on the Narodniks, he underlined, once again, "the determined refusal of Social-Democracy to organise political conspiracies, its emphatic refusal to call the workers to the barricades'...or, in general, to impose on them this or that 'plan' for an attack on the government which has been thought up by a company of revolutionaries..." He called on the Social-Democrats, instead, to "Learn, propagandise and organise". "We do not believe in conspiracies", he repeatedly said, "We renounce individual revolutionary ventures to destroy the government".[16]

What Lenin seems to be saying here is that the workers' movement is not yet ready to launch a mass attack on the government. Therefore, there is a need to carry on propaganda and strengthen the workers' organisation further. Some more remarks that Lenin made later in the same year confirm this interpretation. Discussing what he called "the question of terror", Lenin said: "...in our own personal opinion, terror is *not* advisable as a means of struggle *at the present moment*, that the party (as a party) must renounce it (until there occurs a change of tactics) and concentrate all its energy on organisation and the regular delivery of literature".[17]

Elaborating this viewpoint in 1901 Lenin pointed out that the Russian Social-Democrats had "never rejected" terror in principle, for terror was "one of the forms of...action that may be perfectly suitable and even essential at a definite juncture...given...the existence of definite conditions". Two conditions which, according to him, were essential for the use of terror were: (1) the existence of a "central body" directing the operations; and (2) strong "local revolutionary organisation". Neither of these conditions, asserted Lenin, existed in Russia at the given juncture. The organisation was weak and it lacked "a staff of leaders and organisers". Using terror under such conditions might rupture "the contact between the revolutionary organisations and the disunited masses…"; it might further weaken the already weak organisation by pushing the "most energetic revolutionaries" over to terror. Moreover, according to Lenin, terror could never be "a regular…operation"; at best it could only serve as an "independent form of occasional attack", unconnected with and not integrated into "the entire system of struggle". Lenin, therefore, declared that "under the present conditions" such a means of struggle was "inopportune and unsuitable". The immediate task of the revolutionaries should be to build an organisation "capable of uniting all forces", "ready at any time to support every protest and every outbreak and use it to…consolidate the fighting forces suitable for the decisive struggle…"[18]

Street-fighting and Terrorism

However, in approximately the next one year there was a rapid shift in Lenin's position. As we have seen, he had so far been emphasising on building the organisation that could effectively lead the impending mass struggle against the autocracy. In his writings during the immediately following period, he began to behave, in his statements, as if the time had already come for launching that struggle which was to culminate in a mass armed fight against the regime. This rapid shift in his position was triggered primarily by a clash in the middle of 1901 between the workers of the Obukov Steel Works near St. Petersburg and the police and, later, the army, during which a number of workers were killed. Defending the action of the workers, and condemning those who thought that street-fighting against modern troops was impossible and hopeless, Lenin recalled Engels' words on street-fighting written in 1895 and sarcastically claimed that Engels' views had been distorted by the "wise" bourgeois critics of street-fighting. Insisting that street-fighting was possible, Lenin argued that it was a tactic that "will bring into the foreground more experienced, better armed, and bolder leaders".[19] A few days later, reacting similarly to the claim of the liberals that the struggle against the autocracy could be carried on with peaceful, legal means, Lenin re-emphasised the importance of street-fighting: "...[T]he masses of the workers can obtain *real* political training", he said, "only by their participation in all aspects of the revolutionary movement, including open street-fighting and civil war against the defenders of political and economic slavery".[20] At the same time, Lenin denied that peaceful, legal activity had much role to play in the struggle against the autocracy: "...[T]o include, even indirectly, peaceful, legal activity in the conception of struggle against the autocracy means...to weaken as it is infinitely weak consciousness of the Russian man in the street..."[21]

In March 1902, in a draft resolution written for a conference of the committees and organisations of the Russian Social-Democratic Labour Party, Lenin called on the proletariat to launch an "all-round and nation-wide political agitation". As "practical methods of struggle", he particularly recommended the oragnisation of boycott and mass demonstrations. But he also advised all party committees and groups to devote "due attention to the need for preparatory measures for a nation-wide armed uprising against the autocracy."[22]

Clearly, Lenin has travelled far from his position of 1897 and 1899 when he would not commit himself as to what means were to be employed in the impending struggle against the Russian state. He has now adopted a stance that markedly prefers the violent to the peaceful means. As to the specific means of street-fighting, in 1899 he had emphatically refused to "call the workers to the barricades", but now he openly recommends it. Not only that. He now testifies to the need of preparing for a broad armed uprising against the autocracy.

It is not difficult to see that Lenin conceives even the armed struggle against the autocracy as an open and mass affair, and not a putsch carried out by a band of revolutionaries on the basis of a conspiracy. His views on terrorism in particular and the question of armed struggle in Russia in general continued to be the same up to and during the revolutionary upheaval of 1905.

This period in Russia was one of deep economic crisis. During 1900 to 1903 especially, there was a severe famine which resulted in industrial stagnation and mass unemployment in the cities and a rising discontent in the countryside. The discontent was fanned by the intensifying police repression. These events gave rise to mass strikes and demonstrations both in the cities and the villages. Beginning with 1901, the disturbancc became increasingly violent, frequent and wide spread.[23]

The period saw a resurgence of Narodniks, especially in the countryside, and their reorganisation as the Socialist Revolutionary Party. Following the tactics of their Narodnik days, the Socialist Revolutionaries carried out a number of political murders, the most prominent of which was the assassination of the Minister of Interior, D. S. Sipyagin, in 1902.[24] They justified these tactics by arguing that single acts of terrorism politicised people "more effectively than months of verbal propaganda", and that they infused "new strength into the waverers" etc.[25] At the same time, they claimed that by terrorism they were not "relegating work among the masses into the background". "We advocate terrorism", they said, "not in place of work among the masses, but precisely for and simultaneously with that work."[26]

Lenin, who only a few months ago had given a call for the preparation of mass armed uprising, denounced the terrorism of the Socialist Revolutionaries as "nothing else than single combat", a method that had already been "wholly condemned" by the experience of history. "No verbal assurances and vows", according to him, could disprove "the unquestionable fact" that terrorism as practised by the Socialist Revolutionaries was "not connected in any way" with work among the masses.[27] Single combat, asserted Lenin, "has the immediate effect of creating a short-lived sensation, while indirectly it even leads to apathy and passive waiting for the next bout".[28] By including terrorism in their programme "in its present-day form", Socialist Revolutionaries, therefore, were causing "the most serious harm to the movement, destroying the indissoluble ties between socialist work and the mass of the revolutionary class".[29] Lenin castigated them for their failure to understand that the only hope of the revolution was the masses; that only masses led by a revolutionary organisation could fight against the state. "Without the least denying violence and terrorism in principle", therefore, he demanded work for the preparation of "such forms of violence as were calculated to bring about the direct participation of the masses and which guaranteed that participation".[30]

During the height of revolutionary conflagration, *Revolutionaya Rossiya*, the central organ of the Socialist Revolutionaries, brought up the question of terrorism once again. Writing in connection with the events of January 22, 1905[31] the paper called for the "fusion between terrorism and the mass movement". The paper argued that the separateness of these two factors thus far had "deprived them of their full force".[32] Lenin heartily agreed with the Socialist Revolutionaries. "This is precisely what the revolutionary Social-Democrats have been saying all along", he said. "For this very reason they have always been opposed to terrorism..." He then quoted Plekhanov from an eighteen month old issue of *Iskra* to define his position in precise terms. In his write up, Plekhanov had referred to the "terrorism of the great French Revolution" whose strength was "the strength of the revolutionary movement of the people... *That* terrorism was due, not to disappointment in the strength of the mass movement, but, on the contrary, to unshakable faith in its strength". According to Plekhanov, the history of that terrorism was "exceedingly instructive for the Russian revolutionary". On the basis of this quotation, Lenin reminded the Socialist Revolutionaries of the "importance of faith in the mass movement", only a lack of which led the revolutionaries towards individual terrorism. He asked "the pioneers of the armed struggle" to "submerge" among "the insurgent masses" and proceed with them "in the literal, not figurative symbolical, sense of the word".[33] Military operations "together with the people" was what Lenin meant by the submergence among and proceeding with the people. The time had passed when revolution was "made" by individual revolutionary terrorists. The bomb had ceased to be the weapon of the solitary "bomb thrower", and was becoming "an essential weapon of the people".[34]

We have earlier seen that Lenin had ruled out the use of individual terrorism when the masses had not yet been aroused. He now rules out its use even during the revolutionary upheaval, for when this latter phenomenon is apace, individual terrorism is made redundant by mass violent struggle. Also, we saw earlier that he had asserted that terror could be employed only "in a decisive assault". It can now be argued that mass use of violence during revolution was probably what he had in mind.

So far as the general nature of the struggle against the tsarist government was concerned, the events of January 22, 1905 only strengthened Lenin in his belief that only "an armed people can be the real bulwark of popular liberty".[35] In this connection, Lenin warned the workers against economic concessions that the government had thrown to them as a "sop" immediately after the uprising in order to "save itself", and exhorted them not to forget "the lesson of the Bloody Sunday (January 22)".[36]

Bourgeois-democratic Processes

If we combine Lenin's emphasis, brought out above, on the necessity of a violent revolution under autocratic political conditions with his insistence, pointed out in Chapter 1, that the revolution would remain violent even in bourgeois-democratic states, it should follow that the proletarian movement ought altogether to refrain from using or participating in the bourgeois-democratic processes. This implication also follows from Lenin's belief, to be elaborated shortly, that Russia remained essentially an autocratic state even after the tsar conceded on October 30, 1905 limited constitutional rights to the people in the form of an elected Duma with legislative powers.[37] In practice, however, Lenin's general position with regard to the Duma remained that the revolutionaries must participate in such institutions if only to make use of them for propaganda purposes so far and so long as this was allowed. Nevertheless, tactically there might arise certain periods when it became more advantageous to boycott them completely.

We will illustrate these positions of Lenin by taking first the Duma and later the bourgeois-democratic government which emerged after the March 1917 revolution as examples. But first, we must pause for a brief description of Lenin's view that the Duma did not change the essential character of the Russian state.

We saw in the pages above that according to Lenin there was a divergence of interest between the autocracy and certain strata of the bourgeoisie, and it was this divergence that gave rise to the liberal-bourgeois opposition to the autocracy. In January 1905, he noted that this section of the bourgeoisie was getting increasingly impatient with the autocratic regime "regardless of its fear of the proletariat".[38] In August the same year, he described the coming decision of the tsar to institute a Duma as a "sop to the big bourgeoisie".[39] By instituting the Duma the tsar was accommodating the political interests of the bourgeoisie to an extent greater than ever before. However, the bourgeoisie, while wanting full political freedom for itself, did not want it to be extended to the whole people, because the proletariat could use this freedom against the bourgeoisie. It wanted to retain, therefore, a "number of survivals from the old regime..."[40] pertaining to autocratic administrative and political structures. The Duma, thus, was nothing more than "the instrument of a counter-revolutionary deal between the autocracy and the liberal-monarchist bourgeoisie..."[41] As such, it was extremely important, believed Lenin, to make clear to the people this character of the Duma so that they did not give up their hitherto non-parliamentary struggle under the spell of the newly-created constitutional illusions.[42] Boycott of the Duma at certain moments served this purpose very well.

Boycotting the Duma

The first and the only time Lenin gave a call for the boycott was with regard to the first Duma, the elections for which were held in April 1906. But he did so not without first noting that it "would be ridiculous to renounce" the use of "bourgeois-bureaucratic Duma for puposes of agitation and struggle",[43] and emphasising that "not only a parliament but even a travesty of a parliament may, when the conditions for an uprising are lacking, become the focal point of all our agitation for the entire period when an uprising is out of the question". However, when "an uprising is possible and necessary", then that must become "the central slogan of the whole of our campaign..."[44]

During the period under discussion, Lenin was convinced of both the necessity and the possibility of an uprising. The promised Duma, he believed, was "not a parliament", but "a ruse employed by the autocracy"; it was a "police fraud". Secondly, the rights granted under the manifesto of October 30 were inadequate. The Social-Democratic Party, "the party of the working class", continued to remain illegal. The party , under such conditions, could not "derive any advantage...from the elections".[45] Thirdly, the civil war was still raging. The armed uprising of December 1905[46] showed that the workers had rejected the October manifesto.

Later, in the second half of 1906, Lenin recounted some more reasons why he had asked for the boycott of the first Duma. The call for the boycott was given "at a time when the insurgents were waging an armed fight for a constituent assembly". This was also the time when "the importance of the Duma was being immeasurably exaggerated..." The Cadets (Constitutional Democrats), by making the Duma "the entire basis" of their campaign, were spreading constitutional illusions. At such a time, "*only* by means of boycott could the Social Democrats fulfil their duty of giving people the necessary warning against the tsar's constitution and supplying the necessary criticism of the chicanery of the Cadets during the elections..."[47]

Earlier, when the elections had brought the Cadets into the Duma with a majority,[48] Lenin stuck to the stand he had taken before the elections and insisted that the party must continue to follow its earlier policy. "...[B]y boycotting the state Duma and the Duma elections", he wrote, "the party organisations acted correctly". "...[C]onditions do not yet exist to enable our party to take the parliamentary path".[49]

Every political period, according to him, confronted the Social-Democratic Party, "as the representative of the only thoroughly revolutionary class, with a particular and specific task which becomes the urgent task of the day". The specific political task of the present time was "to combat constitutional illusions".[50] This was so because in Russia there was "nothing like an established, universally-recognised and really parliamentary regime..." Parliament was not "the principal arena of the conflict of social and political interests". The main form of domination of the ruling class in Russia of the day was an "avowedly non-Parliamentary form". Under such circumstances, "insurrection was a reality", while "parliamentarism" was "an unimportant field of struggle".[51]

The dissolution of the Duma by the tsar on July 21 (1906)[52] confirmed, for Lenin, his argument elaborated immediately above. The dissolution had "most strikingly" confirmed, he declared, the views of those who had warned against "being obsessed with the external 'constitutional' aspect of the Duma and...the constitutional surface of Russian politics during the second quarter of 1906". It had exposed the "illusory character of the Russian constitution", and "the fictitious nature of...native parliamentarism..."[53] The objective course of events had shown that the real question of the day was not the question of law, or of the constitution, but the question of power. And the Duma had proved incapable of coping with "the revolutionary task of the struggle for *power*". This task involved "removing, destroying, *overthrowing* the old regime, overthrowing the autocratic government". And in the present period, "The complete achievement of this aim" was "possible only by means of an armed uprising of the whole people".[54]

This did not mean, however, that the Social-Democrats must continue to boycott the Duma in case it is reconvened. At the end of August (1906), Lenin asked them to reconsider the question of boycotting the Duma. While still justifying his call for the boycott of the first Duma given in a definite political situation, Lenin revised his opinion of the Duma in the light of the experience of the immediately preceding months. Experience had shown that when the Duma assembled, opportunities arose for carrying on useful agitation both from within the Duma and around it. History had "ruthlessly confuted" all constitutional illusions, but it had also proved that the institution of the Duma was of "some, although modest" use to the revolution. The time had, therefore, arrived when the Social-Democrats "must cease to be boycottists", but with the understanding that "the Duma campaign is a subordinate and secondary form of struggle, and that, owing to the objective conditions of the moment, direct revolutionary actions by the broad mass of the people still remain the principal form of struggle".[55]

The 'objective conditions' undoubtedly supported Lenin. The dissolution of the Duma had given a fresh impetus to the disturbances that were, by then, slowly receding. It provoked large-scale peasant uprisings and mutinies by the army and naval units. However, these were met with brutal repression by the state, and between the late summer of 1906 and the spring of 1907 more than a thousand executions were officially recorded to have been carried out on the orders of special summary courts-martial established by the government.[56]

Hoping to get a milder Duma in the wake of this repression, the tsar ordered elections for the second Duma. Immediately, Lenin raised the issue of parliamentarism versus armed struggle once again. While accusing the bourgeoisie of trying "to put blinkers on the eyes of the workers", Lenin condemned the anarchists for their inability "to appreciate the historically defined importance of parliamentarism", and for "entirely" renouncing "this method of struggle".[57] The Social-Democrats, in contrast, regarded parliamentarism "as one of the means of enlightening and educating the proletariat and organising it in an independent class party..."[58] They subordinated their parliamentary activities "entirely and absolutely to the general interests of the working class movement...", and did not clamour for parliamentarism "for the sake of parliamentary reforms..."[59] It was not their business to mobilise people for "half-hearted reforms" that were not feasible "without a revolutionary struggle."[60]

This remained Lenin's stance during the period of the third Duma as well. The second Duma, which had assembled in February 1907, was dissolved after three and a half months (June 16). The reason for the dissolution was the refusal by a majority of the members of the Duma to toe the official line. Immediately thereafter, the government changed the election law in order to ensure a preponderance of the conservatives.[61]

An overwhelming majority of the Bolsheviks wanted to boycott the imminent elections to the third Duma, calling it a "cardboard, comic-opera Duma".[62] But Lenin stuck to his previous position and insisted on participation. The Social-Democrats' decision regarding the boycott shoud be determined, he said, not by "the degree of reactionariness" of an institution, but by "the existence of those special conditions of struggle that...make it possible to apply the specific method known as boycott".[63] Boycott was a struggle "not within the framework of a given institution, but against its existence". It was "a refusal to recognise the old regime...", and "a means of struggle aimed at overthrowing the old regime..." To be successful, therefore, the boycott required "a direct struggle against the old regime, an uprising against it and mass disobedience to it in a large number of cases..." The connection between boycott and the broad revolutionary upswing was thus "obvious". Unless there was "mass unrest" which "overflowed the bounds of the old legality", there could be "no question" of the boycott succeeding.[64]

Such conditions had existed, Lenin believed and we have indicated, during 1905 and early 1906. They were now conspicuous by their absence. This was, in Lenin's words, the period of "a temporary lull in the revolution..."[65] It demanded "the humdrum daily work on the humdrum monarchist-constitutional turn". While continuing to work for "a new, broad uprising", therefore, the Social-Democrats must avoid "butting in blindly with the slogan of boycott".[66]

Lenin continued to hold the view sketched above right up to 1914 when the outbreak of the First World War pushed the question of the Duma into the background.

The points that emerge from the above discussion are the following. Whereas by February 1905 Lenin had come to regard armed struggle as the only form of struggle that was likely to succeed under autocratic conditions, from the beginning of 1906 onwards he moved to the position that it was only the primary form of struggle. Obviously, this shift in his position had occurred due to the introduction of the Duma in the Russian political system. The introduction of the Duma made it necessary for the Social-Democrats to adopt parliamentary methods as the auxiliary method of struggle. In other words, when a semi-parliamentary institution had come into existence under an autocratic regime, howsoever temporarily, the use of parliamentary methods could not be avoided. Nevertheless, the mainly autocratic character of the state made it imperative to retain the armed struggle as the primary method. As we have already mentioned, the reasons for the introduction of the Duma were basically economic. Its repeated withdrawal and restructuring also proved the same point. However, as we have explained, its existence had important political and strategic implications for the revolutionary movement.

The Provisional Government

The character of the regime that came into power after the March revolution of 1917 had broadly similar implications for the movement and evoked a more or less similar response from Lenin. The details of the processes that led to the emergence of this regime and its quick downfall have been elaborated elsewhere.[67] Here we shall focus on Lenin's characterisation of the regime in the months immediately following its ascendance into power, as also on the change in tactics that he thought it necessitated.

In Lenin's opinion, after the March revolution the state power in Russia had "passed into the hands of a new class, namely the bourgeoisie and the landowners who had become bourgeois". To that extent, the bourgeois-democratic revolution had been completed. But the old tsarist state had not been "completely destroyed". "The vast landed possessions of the feudalist squirearchy" had not been "abolished", and the loyalists of the monarchy still maintained a powerful political and military existence. The new bourgeois government was attempting to form an alliance with the monarchists, and had already appointed their supporters to certain "key positions". The aim was to "hinder in every way the revolutionary initiative of mass action and the seizure of power by the people *from below*", which was "the sole guarantee of the real success of the revolution". Further, the new government was "for the continuation of the imperialist war", a war that was being waged "in alliance with imperialist powers...for division of the capitalist spoils and for subjugating small and weak nations". For these reasons, Lenin believed, this government did "not deserve the confidence of the proletariat",[68] and must be overthrown. However, it could not be overthrown immediately for three reasons. Firstly, under this government the people enjoyed a number of "legally recognised rights", making Russia "the freest of all the belligerent countries in the world". Secondly, this regime was characterised by an "absence of violence towards the masses". Finally, this government enjoyed, at the moment, the support of the Soviets of Workers' Deputies, which meant, in effect, that a large number of workers were not even hostile to this government.[69]

It was because of these reasons that nearly a month after the revolution, when some of the Bolsheviks raised the question of immediately overthrowing the Provisional Government, Lenin firmly ruled out this course of action. "To become a power the class-conscious workers must win the majority to their side", he wrote. "We are not Blan[quists]",[70] he said, "we do not stand for the seizure of power by a minority".[71] A couple of days later, when a minister in the Provisional Government accused the Bolsheviks of preaching violence, Lenin answered him in the following words: "*Pravda* and its followers do not preach violence. On the contrary, they declare most clearly, precisely and definitely that our efforts should now be concentrated on *explaining* to the proletarian masses their proletarian problems". Continuing in the same vein, Lenin further wrote: "So long as you, capitalist gentlemen...have not yet begun to use violence, it is our tactics...to fight for influence among the proletarian masses" and "the Soviets".[72]

Similarly, in early May 1917, when some newspapers supporting the government alleged that the Bolsheviks were holding out the threat of civil war, Lenin called it a "despicable lie", for "at the present moment", according to him, "any thought of civil war would be naive, senseless" and "preposterous".[73] Next day, on May 6, Lenin repeated these thoughts in a rejoinder to the newspaper *Dyen* which had sarcastically invited the Bolsheviks to "come and take the power". "There is a degree of freedom now in Russia", said Lenin, "that enables the will of the majority to be gauged by the make up of the Soviets. Therefore, to make a serious, not a Blanquist, bid for power, the proletarian party must *fight for influence* within the Soviets".[74] And on May 7, Lenin went a step further and totally withdrew, for the time being, the slogan of converting the 'imperialist' war into a civil war that he had advanced immediately after the start of the First World War.[75]

Lenin seems to have gone back, with these statements, to the pre-war days when he had repeatedly urged the Bolsheviks not to boycott the Duma when no mass upsurge against the government was in sight. A more or less similar situation prevailed now immediately after the March revolution, with the re-emerged Soviets representing the popular mood and working in tandem with the Provisional Government.

Lenin continued to maintain that a socialist revolution even in a bourgeois-democratic state must ultimately be violent, but the precise moment of insurrection must be when conditions were most conducive for its success. Our analysis of Lenin's behaviour in the subsequent period will show that this indeed was the position which he subscribed to right up to the November Revolution. But first, we must explicate his analysis of the First World War and its implications for the Russian revolution.

The War: Imperialist and Civil

The outbreak of the First World War did not, according to Lenin, change the character of the tsarist state, but it caused significant realignment of political forces within Russia. The most important development was the sharpening of polarisation between the bourgeoisie and the liberal-minded landlords on the one hand and the monarchy and the conservative landlords on the other. The war and the enfeeblement of the monarchy that it brought about made it possible for the bourgeoisie to make a thrust for the capture of political power more explicit than had hitherto been possible. Exploiting the defeat of the Russian armies in the first year of the war as a plank, the liberal bourgeoisie, in conjunction with large sections of the conservative bourgeoisie and the liberal landlords, put pressure on the tsar to make "progressive" political reforms in the system. However, the tsar and "the feudal-minded landowners" thought it would be more profitable not to succumb to the pressure and to come to an understanding with the German monarchy instead. This attitude of the tsar and the monarchist landlords led to the second important development that occurred in the wake of the war: the linking up of the domestic Russian situation with the situation in the west.[76]

Both these developments had significant consequences for the nature and direction of the revolutionary socialist movement in Russia. By making the monarchy more vulnerable and its vulnerability more visible, these developments impelled the revolutionary movement, first, to direct its attack more exclusively on the monarchy; secondly, they opened up for this movement the possibility of using violence as an immediate form of struggle against a regime which, embroiled in an international war and linked up with foreign powers, had become a representative of what Lenin called a "military-feudal 'imperialism'".[77] In the context of the subject under consideration, what is important for us is to remember that by isolating the monarchy and by giving its character a military colour, and by thus making possible a violent struggle directed exclusively at the tsar, the war had become a powerful external determinant of the nature and form of revolution inside Russia. In this light, it becomes necessary for us to know in detail Lenin's characterisation of, and attitude towards, the war and the particular form of struggle that it engendered.

Lenin defined this war as a "bourgeois, imperialist and dynastic war". "A struggle for markets and for freedom to loot foreign countries, a striving to suppress the revolutionary movement of the proletariat and democracy in individual countries" and " a desire to deceive, disunite and slaughter the proletarians of all countries by setting the wage slaves of one nation against those of another so as to benefit the bourgeoisie", were, according to him, "the only real content and significance of the war".[78] It followed that the Social-Democrats must organise "an all-embracing propaganda...for...the need to use weapons, not against...brothers, the wage slaves in other countries, but against the reactionary and bourgeois governments and parties of all countries..."[79] The execution of these ideas meant, in effect, the "conversion of the...imperialist war into a civil war", and this, asserted Lenin, was "the only correct proletarian slogan" at the moment. To lend weight to his argument, Lenin evoked the authority of the Stuttgart (1907), Copenhagen (1910), and Basle (1912) resolutions of the Second International, which had anticipated the war as also its 'imperialist' nature, and had called upon the Social-Democrats, in the words of the Stuttgart resolution, "to do all in their power to utilise the economic and political crisis caused by the war to rouse the people and thereby to hasten the abolition of capitalist class rule".[80]

As it turned out, however, a majority of the socialists, both within and outside Russia, supported the war, siding with one or the other of the warring parties, depending upon the country of their origin. In Russia, for example, most of the Mensheviks, including George Plekhanov, and the Socialist Revolutionaries decided to back the

Allies.[81] From the entire socialist movement, Lenin, Rosa Luxemburg and Karl Leibknecht were the only major figures which opposed the war.[82]

Lenin condemned this stance of the socialists everywhere as "betrayal of socialism", and accused them of "rejecting the class struggle with its inevitable conversion at certain moments into civil war".[83] Although this conversion was not an "easy matter", it was, nevertheless, "inherent in the objective conditions of capitalism in general, and of the end of capitalism in particular". The war was not a "chance happening", but "an inevitable stage of capitalism". It was "as legitimate a form of the capitalist way of life as peace is". Unless there was a "series of successful revolutions", this war will soon be followed by others. The horrors of war will not only "intimidate and depress" the proletariat and the semi-proletariat, they will also "enlighten, teach, arouse, organise, steel and prepare" them for the war against the bourgeoisie "of their 'own'...and 'foreign' countries". And this was bound to happen, "if not today, then tomorrow...if not in this war then in the next one".[84]

The essence of Lenin's argument is that sooner or later the war is bound to create an economic and political crisis as well as discontent in the warring countries, and that instead of getting sucked into the nationalist chauvinism that war generally produces, the Social-Democrats should prepare themselves to take advantage of this situation.

However, the international socialist community was not yet ready to accept Lenin's arguments. It displayed its attitude formally in a conference of the international socialists at Zimmerwald (Switzerland) in September 1915 by overwhelmingly rejecting Lenin's resolution which reiterated his call for turning the war into a civil war.[85] A similar resolution moved by Lenin at the Kienthal

(Switzerland) conference of the same group in April 1916, too, met with defeat, although this time it could muster greater support. Also, whereas the Zimmerwald conference had totally rejected such a suggestion, the Kienthal conference declared that "real durable peace" could not be attained without "the conquest of political power...by the peoples themselves".[86] This was fairly close to what Lenin had been saying all along, and what he was to reiterate, in more detail, later in September.

Taking as his starting point Clausewitz's famous statement that war is the continuation of policy by other means, Lenin emphasised that socialists could not afford to "be opposed to all war", and that civil war was "just as much a war as any other".[87] It followed "logically from", and was "dictated by, the whole *objective development* of capitalist militarism".[88] The present "imperialist war" was "the continuation of the imperialist policies of two groups of Great Powers", and these policies were "engendered and fostered by the sum total of the relationship of the imperialist era".[89] Civil war was, therefore, the "natural" and "inevitable, continuation, development and intensification of the class struggle".[90] Only "after" the proletariat had "disarmed the bourgeoisie" will it be able "to consign all armaments to the scrap-heap". Hence the slogan of the proletariat to defeat, expropriate and disarm the bourgeoisie.[91]

Revolutionary Situation

If we accept Lenin's analysis of the 'imperialist' war as valid, the tactic of civil war at the domestic level seems to be, during the period of the war, a logical and practical necessity. But what was, according to him, the exact nature of the situation which the war had created? How did this situation make recourse to violent methods of struggle and civil war inevitable?

Writing in May-June 1915, about the 'collapse' of the Second International, Lenin defined this situation as a "revolutionary situation" and elaborated its precise characteristics. To a Marxist it was "indisputable", he added, that a revolution was "impossible" without a revolutionary situation, though not "every" revolutionary situation led to revolution. A revolutionary situation had three major symptoms. One, "when it is impossible for the ruling classes to maintain their rule without any change". At such a time, there is a "crisis, in one form or another", in the policy of the ruling classes. This crisis leads to "a fissure through which the discontent and indignation of the oppressed classes burst forth". Two, "when the suffering and want of the oppressed classes have grown more acute than usual". The third symptom is a "consequence" of the above causes. It is constituted of "a considerable increase in the activity of the masses, who uncomplainingly allow themselves to be robbed in 'peace time', but in turbulent times, are drawn both by all the circumstances of the crisis and by the *'upper classes' themselves into independent historical action*". "Without these objective changes", emphasised Lenin, "which are independent of the will, not only of individual groups and parties, but even of individual classes, a revolution as a general rule is impossible". The "totality" of these objective changes is what is called a revolutionary situation.[92]

Such a situation existed, according to Lenin, in Russia in 1905 although no revolution took place at that time. This was so because "revolution arises only out of a situation in which the above-mentioned objective changes are accompanied by a subjective change, namely, the ability of the revolutionary *class* to take revolutionary mass action *strong* enough to break (or dislocate) the old government, which never, not even in a period of crisis, 'falls' if it is not toppled over".[93]

Implied in Lenin's emphasis on the necessity of subjective changes accompanying the objective changes for the emergence of the revolution was the assertion that such changes had not yet taken place in Russia. Explicitly, this assertion gets manifested through his exhortation to "all socialists" to take it as their "indisputable duty" to reveal "to the masses the existence of a revolutionary situation, explaining its scope and depth, arousing the proletariat's revolutionary consciousness and revolutionary determination" and "helping it go over to revolutionary action..."[94]

It is clear that, according to Lenin, a revolutionary situation existed in Russia, but he was not sure regarding the ability of the proletariat to make a revolution. We have to conclude, therefore, that by urging the Social-Democrats to turn the war into a civil war he was endeavouring to hasten the formation of 'subjective' conditions in the already existing revolutionary situation.

However, the existence of even these subjective conditions was not sufficient, believed Lenin, when it came to determining the precise moment of the insurrection. If the insurrection had to be successful, the determination of this moment must be based on the existence of three further conditions. These three conditions were: (1) the insurrection must not rely upon a conspiracy and a party but on an "advanced class"; (2) the insurrection must be attempted at the time of a "revolutionary upsurge" among the people; and (3) the attempt must coincide with that "turning point" in the history of the "growing revolution" when the activity of the advanced class is at its height, and when the "vacillations" in the ranks of the "weak, half-hearted and irresolute friends of the revolution are strongest".[95] These conditions had emerged, in his view, particularly after the famous July 17 (1917) demonstration against the government by half-a-million workers and armed soldiers, and the September (7-10) revolt by General Kornilov.[96] Another development which had precipitated these conditions was the failure of the Soviets to assemble all power in their own hands, as Lenin had initially hoped that they would, and their cession of most of the power to the Provisional Government,[97] thus putting an end to the phenomenon of "dual power", pointed out by Lenin in April 1917, under which the proletariat's support to the government was justified by him till such time as the Soviets had taken full possession of state power.[98] These conditions, coupled with the fact that ever since the March revolution the Provisional Government had become increasingly authoritarian and anti-people,[99] prompted Lenin to withdraw the slogan "All Power to the Soviets" which he had advanced in April and give a call for an immediate armed seizure of power.[100]

In the subsequent days, Lenin repeatedly asked the central committee to launch the insurrection immediately,[101] but the committee judged the situation differently. It was sure of victory only in Moscow and Petersburg, and not at all in provinces.[102] Therefore, it stubbornly kept rejecting Lenin's call. Even after Lenin was able, on October 23, to get his line approved, and the central committee agreed, in principle, that the time was ripe for insurrection, it kept delaying action so that on November 6, the day the insurrection was started, Lenin still had to prod the committee with a sharp letter.[103]

The immediate success of the venture proved that Lenin had been right about the timing of the insurrection. The soldiers and workers who went into action on behalf of the Bolsheviks met with little resistance, and the capture of power was almost bloodless.[104] But this was only in Petersburg and to some extent in Moscow. The fact that the Bolsheviks had to wage a long and bloody war before they could finally win the sprawling countryside, testifies that the doubting members of the central committee too had been right. So that we can neither accuse Lenin of running ahead of the events nor condemn the rest of the leading Bolsheviks for lagging behind.

Suppressing the Bourgeoisie

We have seen in Chapter 1 that according to Lenin the existence of democratic, parliamentary institutions did not at all ensure that a socialist revolution could be made in a peaceful manner. And in the present chapter we saw that in the context of Russia this remained Lenin's attitude, first, towards the semi-parliamentary institution, the Duma, and later towards the bourgeois-democratic regime that emerged there after the overthrow of the tsar. We also saw that throughout the period that the Duma and the Provisional Government regime existed, Lenin justified his revolutionary strategy in the context of these institutions through his analysis of the events connected with them—a strategy that insisted on the use of violent and peaceful methods alternatively but with the proviso that in the final analysis the Bolsheviks could not capture power without using violent means. Finally, we saw that on Lenin's insistence the Bolsheviks did effect a violent—and if we take the long civil war into account, a bloody—capture of power.

We will now briefly show that Lenin did not change his belief and attitude in the subsequent years. These years were devoted, on the one hand, to the destruction of those feudal-bourgeois state structures which the Bolsheviks had inherited, and, on the other, to the building of the socialist state.

So far as the destruction of the inherited state structures is concerned, Lenin had made clear his general position on this issue in August-September 1917 itself, that is, even before the November Revolution, when he wrote his well-known book *The State and Revolution*. In this book, he had elaborated what he claimed was the Marxist theory of state, but the real purpose of the book was to discuss "the question of the relation of the socialist proletarian revolution to the state", which was "acquiring not only practical political importance, but also the significance of a most urgent problem of the day".[105] This book contains the first coherent theoretical justification of the use of violence in a socialist revolution during the phase of the dictatorship of the proletariat. Although Marx and Engels too, we have seen, selectively justified this use throughout their writings, they had never exclusively focused on this subject, nor had they ever elaborated it with such emphasis and in such detail. This theoretical coherence had also not been a feature of Lenin's own utterances on this subject thus far. However, since the essential argument of the book has already been outlined before,[106] we shall elaborate below only those statements of Lenin which he made subsequent to the November Revolution and in the context of the ongoing process of revolution.

Throughout the *The State and Revolution*, Lenin had contended, quoting Marx and Engels, that the bourgeois class had to be suppressed during the dictatorship of the proletariat. After the victory of the Bolsheviks in November 1917, the Russian revolution, according to him, had entered that phase. Accordingly, on November 19, he asked the Bolsheviks to "Establish the strictest revolutionary law and order" and to "mercilessly suppress" any attempts to "create anarchy".[107]

When the Bolsheviks were accused of terrorism and violence, Lenin replied that the resistance of the propertied classes had to be "crushed". We will use "the same means", he said, "as they used to crush the proletariat—no other means have been invented".[108] "Nobody, with the exception of the utopian socialists", had "ever asserted", he declared, "that vicotry" was "possible—without seizing the old world in an iron grip".[109] The Marxists had "always known, said and emphasised that socialism takes shape in the course of the most intense, the most acute class struggle—which reaches heights of frenzy and desperation—and civil war..." They had "always said" that "a special state (that is, a special system of organised coercion of a definite class) corresponds to the transitional period between the bourgeois and the socialist society…" This state "implies and means…a state of simmering war" and of "military measures…against the enemies of the proletarian power". Lenin recalled, in this connection, the "reproach" of Marx and Engels to the Communards of 1871 for not having used their armed force "with *sufficient* vigour" to suppress the resistance of the old classes. And he assured his critics that the resistance to the revolution "*will* be broken" by "systematic application of *coercion* to an entire class (the bourgeoisie) and its accomplices".[110]

To give effect to these ideas, Lenin ensured the institution (through the Congress of the Soviets, on January 25, 1918) of a "universal labour conscription" on the one hand, and "the arming of the working people…and the complete disarming of the propertied classes…" on the other.[111] Further, by a resolution of the All Russia Executive Committee, on January 16, it was declared that "any attempt by any person…to usurp any of the functions of the state power will be regarded as a counter-revolutionary act", and "will be suppressed by every means…including the use of armed force".[112] On January 20, Lenin argued that even the "passive and covert" resistance of the bourgeoisie and its supporters must "definitely" be "crushed".[113] And on February 6, he exhorted the Bolsheviks to expropriate what he called the "plundered goods" of the former ruling classes. "The people must ferret out the sharks and make them disgorge". They "must get at them in their hideouts". They must not wait for the police, but must "themselves…do this".[114]

In August 1918, Lenin was still urging the proletariat on, and was regretting that the task was not being carried out "with sufficient firmness and determination".[115] In November, he picked up a controversy over this issue with Kautsky who had contended that the dictatorship of the proletariat was not a major concept in Marx's doctrine as it rested "upon a single word…which Marx once used in 1875 in a letter". Secondly, according to Kautsky, by dictatorship here Marx did not mean a dictatorship "in the literal sense of the term"; he spoke of "a *condition*" rather than "a form of government". This was "proved by the fact that he was of the opinion that in Britain and America the transition might take place peacefully, i.e., in a democratic way". Kautsky added that Marx had "unfortunately, neglected to show us in greater detail how he conceived this dictatorship…"[116] On the basis of this argument, Kautsky made a distinction between "the two socialist trends" in the Soviet Union, the Bolsheviks and the non-Bolsheviks. The contrast between them was "the contrast between two radically different methods: the *dictatorial* and the *democratic*".[117]

Lenin retaliated by saying that Kautsky was talking like the liberals, speaking of democracy "in general, and not of bourgeois democracy…" The dictatorship of the proletariat, according to him, was "the very essence of Marx's doctrine…" Further, the formula "dictatorship of the proletariat" was "merely a more historically concrete and scientifically exact formulation of the proletariat's task of 'smashing' the bourgeois state machine, about which both Marx and Engels…spoke for forty years, between 1852 and 1891".[118] Then he gave his own definition of dictatorship, which, he said, "is the rule based directly upon force and unrestricted by any laws". And the "revolutionary dictatorship of the proletariat" was the "rule won and maintained by the use of force of violence by the proletariat against the bourgeoisie, rule that is unrestricted by any laws".[119] Clarifying these statements, he added: "[D]ictatorship does not necessarily mean the abolition of democracy for the class that exercises the dictatorship over other classes; but it does mean the abolition…of democracy for the class over which, or against which, the dictatorship is exercised".[120] To draw a distinction between the 'condition' and the 'form' of government, as Kautsky had done, he emphasised, was "a crude falsification of Marx who was clearly speaking here of this or that type of *state*, and not forms of government", as all forms of government under capitalism "are only variations of the *bourgeois state*, that is, the *dictatorship of the bourgeoisie*". So far as England and America were concerned, he repeated his point made earlier in *The State and Revolution* that there was a need to use violence even in these countries because of their "militarism and bureaucracy", institutions "that were non-existent" there "in the seventies".[121]

A look at the relevant statements of Marx and Engels reveals Kautsky to be on a weak ground. Marx and Engels spoke of the dictatorship of the proletariat not on one but many occasions between 1852 and 1883, and , in the context of continental Europe, they clearly stated that the task of the proletariat during this phase of the revolution was to "smash" (Marx) the bourgeois state apparatus and to "stamp out" (Engels) the resistance of the bourgeoisie. Obviously, these acts cannot be accomplished in the absence of a dictatorial proletarian state. With regard to England and America, both Kautsky and Lenin seem to be misrepresenting Marx. As we have seen in Chapter 1, in both these countries the development of the revolution, *after* the workers had won power through parliamentary means, could, according to Marx, be either peaceful or violent depending upon how the old ruling classes reacted to the changes that the working class may make in the structures of the state.

For the next one year, Lenin continued to defend the particular conception of the dictatorship of the proletariat he had elaborated before and during his controversy with Kautsky.[122] In December 1919, he assigned to this dictatorship a task he had hitherto never discussed, that of becoming "an instrument for winning to the side of the proletariat the *non-proletarian working masses...*" (emphasis added). This was to be done "*by satisfying their most urgent economic needs in a revolutionary way*", that is, "*by expropriating the landowners and the bourgeoisie*".[123]

In July 1920, Lenin added some more tasks to the one mentioned above. One was "to neutralise, or render harmless, the inevitable vacillation between the bourgeoisie and the proletariat...to be seen in the class of petty proprieters in agriculture, industry and commerce...as well as in the stratum of intellectuals, salary earners, etc..." This task required, according to him, "a skilful, timely and flexible combination" of the methods of coercion and conciliation. Another was "overcoming the inevitable resistance of that small minority, the *labour aristocracy*, who have been corrupted by capitalism, the old trade union and co-operative leaders etc..." Lenin also talked of exposing and intensifying the struggle against "all groups, parties and leaders in the *working-class movement* who have fully or partly adopted the stand of reformism", for by doing this they "side with the bourgeoisie or join the waverers, or else land in the ranks of the unreliable friends of the victorious proletariat" (emphasis added).[124]

It is clear that for Lenin the tasks of the dictatorship of the proletariat were not limited to suppressing or eliminating the bourgeoisie and the landlords. The dictatorship was also to be used to neutralise all those belonging to the non-bourgeois, non-landlord classes who would oppose in any way the interests of the proletariat for whatever reasons. These could include the members of the working class as well.

NOTES

[1] Lenin, "On the so-called Market Question", *Collected Works*, Volume 1, Foreign Languages Publishing House, Moscow, 1960, pp. 109-12.

[2] Lenin, "What the 'Friends of the People' Are and How They Fight the Social Democrats", *Collected Works*, ibid., p. 197.

[3] Ibid., pp. 245, 264 and 270.

[4] Lenin, "The Economic Content of Narodnism and the Criticism of It in Mr. Struve's Book", *Collected Works*, ibid., pp. 374-75.

[5] Ibid., pp. 377-78 and 465.

[6] Lenin, "Draft and Explanation of a Programme for the Social-Democratic Party", *Collected Works*, Volume 2, Foreign Languages Publishing House, Moscow, 1960, pp. 95 and 99-100.

[7] Ibid., p. 101.

[8] Ibid., pp. 110-11. Also see "Capitalism in Agriculture", *Collected Works*, Volume 4, Foreign Languages Publishing House, Moscow, 1960, pp. 150-59.

[9] Lenin, "Draft and Explanation of a Programme for the Social-Democratic Party", *Collected Works*, Volume 2, op. cit., pp. 110-11.

[10] Lenin, "Political Agitation and 'the Class Point of View'", *Collected Works*, Volume 5, Foreign Languages Publishing House, Moscow, 1961, pp. 339-40; "A Letter to the Northern League", *Collected Works*, Volume 6, Foreign Languages Publishing House, Moscow, 1961, p. 164; and "From Narodnism to Marxism", *Collected Works*, Volume 8, Foreign Languages Publishing House, Moscow, 1962, pp. 87-89.

[11] Lenin, "The Economic Content of Narodnism", *Collected Works*, Volume 1, op. cit., p. 467.

[12] Lenin, "Draft Programme for the Russian Social-Democratic Labour Party", *Collected Works*, Volume 6, op. cit., pp. 29-30.

[13] Lenin, "The Tasks of the Russian Social-Democrats", *Collected Works*, Volume 2, op. cit., p. 342.

[14] Ibid., p. 340.

[15] Ibid., pp. 340-41.

[16] Lenin, "Our Immediate Task", *Collected Works*, Volume 4, op. cit., pp. 217-18 and 220.

[17] Lenin, "A Draft Programme of Our Party", *Collected Works*, ibid., p. 238. Emphases, unless otherwise indicated, are in the original.

[18] Lenin, "Where to Begin", *Collected Works*, Volume 5, op. cit., pp. 19-20.

[19] Lenin, "Another Massacre", *Collected Works*, ibid., p. 29.

[20] See footnote to the article "Persecutors of Zemstvo and Hannibals of Liberalism", *Collected Works*, ibid., p. 68.

[21] Ibid., p. 67.

[22] Lenin, "Report of the *Iskra* Editorial Board to the Meeting (Conference) of R.S.D.L.P. Committees", *Collected Works*, Volume 6, op. cit., pp. 105-06.

[23] See *Lenin: A Biography*, Progress Publishers, Moscow, 1983, p. 75; Leonard Schapiro, *The Communist Party of Soviet Union*, Eyre and Spottiswoode, London, 1960, pp. 39-40; and Edward Crankshaw, *The Shadow of the Winter Palace: The Drift to Revolution*, Macmillan London Limited, London and Basingstoke, 1976, p. 314.

[24] See Adam B. Ulam, *Lenin and the Bolsheviks*, Fontana/Collins, Glasgow, 1977, p. 224; G. D. H. Cole, *The Second International, 1889-1964*, Part I, Macmillan & Co. Ltd., London, 1956, pp. 430-31; Lionel Kochan and Richard Abraham, *The Making of Modern Russia*, Penguin Books, Harmondsworth, 1983, p. 245; and Crankshaw, op. cit., p. 317.

[25] Quoted by Lenin in "Why the Social-Democrats Must Declare A Determined and Relentless War on the Socialist-Revolutionaries", *Collected Works*, Volume 6, op. cit., p. 175.

[26] Quoted by Lenin in "Revolutionary Adventurism", *Collected Works*, ibid., pp. 189-90.

[27] Lenin, "Why the Social-Democrats Must Declare A Determined and Relentless War on the Socialist-Revolutionaries", *Collected Works*, ibid., p. 175.

[28] Lenin, "Revolutionary Adventurism", *Collected Works*, ibid., p. 193.

[29] Lenin, "Why the Social-Democrats Must Declare A Determined and Relentless War on the Socialist-Revolutionaries", *Collected Works*, ibid., p. 175.

[30] Lenin, "Revolutionary Adventurism", *Collected Works*, ibid., p. 195.

[31] On this day a peaceful procession of about 1,50,000 unarmed workers, heading towards the tsar's palace in order to present a petition there, was brutally dispersed by the military. Approximately a thousand people were killed and many thousands wounded. See Ulam, op. cit., pp. 264-65; Kochan and Abraham, op. cit., pp. 249-50; *Lenin: A Biography*, op. cit., pp. 111-12; Schapiro, op. cit., pp. 64-65; and Cole, op. cit., pp. 446-48.

[32] Quoted by Lenin in "A Militant Agreement for the Uprising", *Collected Works*, Volume 8, op. cit., p. 160.

[33] Lenin, ibid., pp. 160-62.

[34] Lenin, "From the Defensive to the Offensive", *Collected Works*, Volume 9, Foreign Languages Publishing House, Moscow, 1962, p. 284.

[35] Lenin, "The Beginning of the Revolution in Russia", *Collected Works*, Volume 8, op. cit., p. 99.

[36] Ibid., p. 98.

[37] For the details on this issue, see Cole, op. cit., p. 457; Bertram Wolfe, *The Three Who Made a Revolution*, The Dial Press, New York, 1948, pp. 321-22; and Robert Conquest, *Lenin*, Fontana/Collins, Glasgow, 1976, p. 54.

[38] Lenin, "From Narodnism to Marxism", *Collected Works*, Volume 8, op. cit., p. 88.

[39] Lenin, "Oneness of the Tsar and the People, and of the People and the Tsar", *Collected Works*, Volume 9, op. cit., p. 191.

[40] Lenin, "The Fight for Power and the 'Fight' for Sops", *Collected Works*, Volume 11, Foreign Languages Publishing House, Moscow, 1962, p. 28.

[41] Ibid., pp. 79-80.

[42] Lenin, "Draft Resolutions for the Fifth Congress of the R.S.D.L.P.", *Collected Works*, Volume 12, Foreign Languages Publishing House, Moscow, 1962, p. 140.

[43] Lenin, "The Boycott of the Bulygin Duma, and Insurrection", *Collected Works*, Volume 9, op. cit., p. 182.

[44] Ibid., p. 273.

[45] Lenin, "Should We Boycott the State Duma?", *Collected Works*, Volume 10, Foreign Languages Publishing House, Moscow, 1962, p. 98.

[46] The uprising was staged by the workers of Moscow and lasted for nine continuous days. See Kochan and Abraham, op. cit., pp. 251, 254-55 and 264; Ulam, op. cit., pp. 292-93, 297 and 304-09; *Lenin: A Biography*, op. cit., pp. 124 and 130-31; and Schapiro, op. cit., pp. 65-70.

[47] Lenin, "The Boycott", *Collected Works*, Volume 11, op. cit., pp. 141-44.

[48] See Cole, op. cit., pp. 467-69; and Schapiro, op. cit., pp. 83-84.

[49] Lenin, "The Unity Congress of the R.S.D.L.P.", *Collected Works*, Volume 10, op. cit., pp. 292-93.

[50] Ibid., p. 273.

[51] Lenin, "Victory of the Cadets and the Tasks of the Workers' Party", *Collected Works*, ibid., p. 235.

[52] See Schapiro, op. cit., p. 90; and Crankshaw, op. cit, pp. 364-65.

[53] Lenin, "The Dissolution of the Duma and the Tasks of the Proletariat", *Collected Works*, Volume 11, op. cit., pp. 111-12

[54] Ibid., pp. 117-18.

[55] Lenin, "The Boycott", *Collected Works*, ibid., pp. 145-48.

[56] See Cole, op. cit., pp. 469-70; and Crankshaw, op. cit., p. 366.

[57] Lenin, "The Social-Democrats and Electoral Agreements", *Collected Works*, Volume 11, op. cit., p. 278.

[58] Ibid., p. 277.

[59] Ibid., p. 278.

[60] Lenin, "The Fifth Congress of the Russian Social-Democratic Labour Party", *Collected Works*, Volume 12, op. cit., p. 487.

[61] See Cole, op. cit., pp. 476-77; Crankshaw, op. cit., p. 370; Wolfe, op. cit., pp. 358-59; and Ulam, op. cit., p. 345.

[62] Quoted in Wolfe, op. cit., p. 359.

[63] Lenin, "Against the Boycott", *Collected Works*, Volume 13, Foreign Languages Publishing House, Moscow, 1962, p. 18.

[64] Ibid., pp. 24-25.

[65] Ibid., p. 36.

[66] Ibid., p. 34.

[67] See, in particular, Tony Cliff, *All Power to the Soviets*, Bookmarks, London, 1985, pp. 27-31 and 77-82; Kochan and Abraham, op. cit., p. 286; Julius Braunthal, *History of the International*, Volume 2, 1914-1943, Thomas Nelson and Sons, London, 1967, p. 65; and G. D. H. Cole, *Communism and Democracy*, 1914-1931, Macmillan and Co. Ltd., London, 1961, p. 69.

[68] Lenin, "The Tasks of the Proletariat in Our Revolution", *Collected Works*, Volume 24, Progress Publishers, Moscow, 1964, pp. 57-58.

[69] Lenin, "The Tasks of the Proletariat in the Present Revolution", and "The Dual Power", *Collected Works*, ibid., pp. 22 and 40 respectively.

[70] In the original text this word has been printed, wrongly in our view, as 'Blancists'. See "The Dual power", ibid., p. 40.

[71] Ibid.

[72] Lenin, "A Shameless Lie of the Capitalists", *Collected Works*, ibid., pp. 110-11.

[73] Lenin, "Resolution of the Central Committee of the R.S.D.L.P. (Bolsheviks)", *Collected Works*, ibid., p. 201.

[74] Lenin, "How a Simple Question can be Confused", *Collected Works*, ibid., p. 217.

[75] Lenin, "The Seventh (April) All-Russian Conference of the R.S.D.L.P. (B.)", *Collected Works*, ibid., pp. 236-37.

[76] Lenin, "The Defeat of Russia and the Revolutionary Crisis", *Collected Works*, Volume 21, Progress Publishers, Moscow, 1964, pp. 378-80.

[77] Lenin, "The Defeat of Russia and the Revolutionary Crisis", "Several Theses", and "On the Two Lines in the Revolution", *Collected Works*, ibid., pp. 381, 402, and 420 respectively.

[78] Lenin, "The Tasks of Revolutionary Social-Democracy in the European War", *Collected Works*, ibid., pp. 15-16.

[79] Ibid., p. 18.

[80] Lenin, quoted in Tony Cliff, op. cit., p. 2.

[81] See Braunthal, op. cit., pp. 31-33; and Cole, *Communism and Democracy*, op. cit., pp. 63-64.

[82] See Cliff, op. cit., pp. 2-3; Braunthal, op. cit., pp. 1-30; Ulam, op. cit., pp. 394-96; and Conquest, op. cit., pp. 72-73.

[83] Lenin, "The Tasks of Revolutionary Social-Democracy in the European War", *Collected Works*, Volume 21, op. cit., pp. 16-17.

[84] Lenin, "The Position and the Tasks of the Socialist-International", *Collected Works*, ibid., pp. 39-40.

[85] See Cliff, op. cit., pp. 12-13; Braunthal, op. cit., pp. 47-49; and Cole, *Communism and Democracy*, op. cit., pp. 77-78.

[86] See Cole, ibid., p. 36.

[87] Lenin, "The Military Programme of the Proletarian Revolution", *Collected Works*, Volume 23, Progress Publishers, Moscow, 1964, pp. 77-78.

[88] Ibid., p. 81.

[89] Ibid., p. 80.

[90] Ibid., p. 78.

[91] Ibid., p. 81.

[92] Lenin, "The Collapse of the Second International", *Collected Works*, Volume 21, op. cit., pp. 213-14.

[93] Ibid., p. 214.

[94] Ibid., pp. 216-17.

[95] For details, see Lenin, "Marxism and Insurrection", *Collected Works*, Volume 26, Progress Publishers, Moscow, 1964, pp. 22-23 and 25.

[96] For details relating to these issues, see Cliff, op. cit., pp. 264, 272-76 and 294-304.

[97] Ibid., pp. 84-96.

[98] Lenin, "The Tasks of the Proletariat in Our Revolution", *Collected Works*, Volume 24, op. cit., pp. 60-71.

[99] Lenin, "The Seventh (April) All-Russian Conference of the R.S.D.L.P. (B.)", and "The Petty-Bourgeois Stand on the Question of Economic Disorganisation", *Collected Works*, Volume 24, ibid., pp. 275-76 and 563-74 respectively.

[100] Lenin, "Marxism and Insurrection", *Collected Works*, Volume 26, op. cit., pp. 22-23 and 25.

[101] Lenin, "The Crisis has Matured", "Letter to the Central Committee, the Moscow and Petrograd Committees and Bolshevik Members of the Petrograd and Moscow Soviets", and "Advice of the Onlooker", *Collected Works*, Volume 26, ibid., pp. 84, 140-41 and 179-81, respectively.

[102] See N. Bukharin, quoted in Cliff, op. cit., p. 339.

[103] Lenin, "Letter to Central Committee Members", *Collected Works*, Volume 26, op. cit., pp. 234-35.

[104] See Kochan and Abraham, op. cit., p. 304.

[105] Lenin, Preface to the first edition of "The State and Revolution", in *Collected Works*, Volume 25, Progress Publishers, Moscow, 1964, p. 384.

[106] See, in particular, Lucio Colletti, in Robin Blackburn, ed., *Revolution and Class Struggle: A Reader in Marxist Politics*, Fontana/Collins, Glasgow, 1977, pp. 69-77. See also, Rustam Singh, "Restoring Revolutionary Theory: Towards an Understanding of Lenin's *The State and Revolution*", *Economic and Political Weekly*, Bombay, Vol. XXIV, No. 43 (October 26, 1989).

[107] Lenin, "To the Population", *Collected Works*, Volume 26, op. cit., p. 297.

[108] Lenin, "Speech on the Constituent Assembly", in the Meeting of the All-Russia Central Executive Committee, December 1 (14), 1917, *Collected Works*, ibid., p. 354.

[109] Lenin, "Speech on the Nationalisation of the Banks", delivered at a Meeting of the All-Russia Central Executive Committee, December 14 (27), 1917, *Collected Works*, ibid., p. 389.

[110] Lenin, "Fear of the Collapse of the Old and the Fight for the New", *Collected Works*, ibid., p. 402.

[111] Lenin, "Declaration of Rights of the Working and Exploited People", *Collected Works*, ibid., p. 424.

[112] Lenin, "Resolution of the All-Russia Central Executive Committee", January 3 (16), 1918, *Collected Works*, ibid., p. 428.

[113] Lenin, "On the History of the Question of the Unfortunate Peace", *Collected Works*, ibid., p. 443.

[114] Lenin, "Speech to the Propagandists on Their Way to the Provinces", January 23 (February 6), 1918, *Collected Works*, ibid., p. 516.

[115] Lenin, *The Socialist Revolution*, Progress Publishers, Moscow, 1981, p. 302.

[116] Quoted by Lenin, ibid., pp. 308-09.

[117] Quoted by Lenin, ibid., p. 307.

[118] Ibid., pp. 308-09.

[119] Ibid., p. 311.

[120] Ibid., p. 310.

[121] Ibid., pp. 312-13.

[122] See articles, "'Democracy' and 'Dictatorship'", "First Congress of the Communist International, March 2-6, 1919", "Rough Draft of the Programme of the RCP(B)", and "Draft Programme of the RCP (Bolsheviks)", in Lenin, *On the Dictatorship of the Proletariat*, Progress Publishers, Moscow, 1982.

[123] Ibid., pp. 225 and 227.

[124] Ibid., pp. 323 and 325.

4

Inevitability of Violence: Underdeveloped Capitalism and the Feudal-colonial State

We concluded in Chapter 3 that Lenin was in agreement with Marx and Engels insofar as he believed, like them, that the nature of the political institutions was determined by the economic structures, but he deviated from their position when he asserted that a socialist revolution will have to be violent in all cases because, in his view, all pre-socialist political institutions, including the capitalist political institutions, remained essentially authoritarian. He argued that in the case of autocratic political conditions in particular, which are the product of feudal economic structures and may linger when the capitalist economic structures have already started to emerge, a violent socialist revolution becomes all the more inevitable. Carrying his analysis beyond domestic borders, he pointed out imperialist war as an additional factor that was responsible for making a socialist revolution violent. The imperialist war played this role by giving a further tilt towards authoritarianism/autocratism to feudal or capitalist political institutions. But if we leave aside the bourgeois-democratic societies and consider only those societies which had undiluted authoritarian/autocratic political institutions, it is clear that Lenin only followed the argument of Marx and Engels and extended it further.

We have, once again, already seen in Chapter 1 that Mao is closer to Lenin than to Marx and Engels in so far as he believed that ultimately a violent socialist revolution was inevitable even in societies with bourgeois parliamentary institutions. When we come to predominantly feudal societies with authoritarian political institutions, we find that here too Mao's position was not much different from that of Lenin. As we shall see in the present chapter, Mao believed that a socialist revolution in a predominantly feudal society like China will be inevitably violent because of mainly two reasons: (1) the unremitting oppression under feudal conditions will force the masses to react in a violent manner; and (2) the power of the feudal forces was so deeply entrenched that it could not be overthrown without the use of violence. Mao stayed close to the position of Lenin in one more respect. In a manner not very dissimilar to that of Lenin, he regarded the direct or indirect presence of imperialist forces as one of the important factors that contributed to the necessity of a violent socialist revolution in a predominantly feudal society. In this respect, he differed from Lenin in only one way. Whereas for Lenin it was a full-scale imperialist war that exacerbated the inevitability of a violent revolution, for Mao even the presence of imperialist political and/or military forces was sufficient to create a situation which left no option with the socialists except waging a violent struggle.

In China the presence of the imperialist military forces led to a situation which was specifically instrumental in taking Mao away from Lenin so far as the form of the revolutionary struggle is concerned. As we know, for Lenin the form of the struggle that the authoritarian conditions made inevitable was that of a civil war. While Mao too advocated this form when the struggle was directed against the feudal classes in a purely domestic context, or when it was directed against imperialist powers when they were working indirectly through their domestic class agents, he asserted that the struggle will have to be waged as a regular military war in the event an imperialist power physically occupied a part or whole of China in collaboration with the comprador classes. This idea of a regular military war as a method of revolutionary struggle was his original contribution to the Marxist theory of revolution. It was a product of the peculiar economic and political situation in China during the years Mao developed his thought.

We begin our exposition with Mao's characterisation of this situation.

Feudal-colonial State

Like Marx's and Engels' in the case of continental western Europe and Lenin's in the case of Russia, Mao's characterisation of the Chinese economy and state did not remain uniform throughout his political career. During the period from March 1926 to October 1928 he characterised the Chinese economy and state as semi-feudal, semi-colonial and marginally capitalist. Accordingly, the classes that were dominant were the feudal landlords, military warlords and two sections of the bourgeoisie, the big bourgeoisie and the national bourgeoisie. Among these the two former and the big bourgeoisie were the agents of the indirect imperialist rule, whereas the last one, that is, the national bourgeoisie, was anti-imperialist, but at the same time also anti-working class, a trait which it shared with the big bourgeoisie.

Analysing the character of these classes in March 1926, Mao described the landlord class, the warlords and the big bourgeoisie as "wholly appendages of the international bourgeoisie, depending upon imperialism for their survival and growth".[1] These classes represented the "most backward and most reactionary relations of production in China" and hindered the development of her productive forces. The big landlords and the big bourgeoisie in particular always sided with imperialism and constituted an extremely counter-revolutionary group. Their existence, therefore, was "utterly incompatible with the aims of the Chinese revolution".[2]

The national bourgeoisie, on the other hand, was "inconsistent" in its attitude towards the Chinese revolution. It felt the need for revolution and favoured the revolutionary movement against imperialism and the warlords, but was, simultaneously, suspicious of the revolution, for it sensed that the revolution threatened its hope "to attain the status of a big bourgeoisie". Nevertheless, its aim remained the establishment of a state under its own rule.[3]

Mao's characterisation of the national bourgeoisie outlined immediately above and his belief, mentioned earlier, that it was one of the dominant classes in the Chinese society could suggest that he wanted the revolutionary movement to treat the national bourgeoisie as an enemy class as a matter of immediate necessity. In reality, Mao's understanding of the stage of the Chinese revolution led him to defer the revolutionary hostility against the national bourgeoisie for the time being. In October 1928 and again in November of the same year, he agreed with the Communist International that China was "still at the stage of the bourgeois-democratic revolution" and that the programme for such a revolution comprised "externally, the overthrow of imperialism so as to achieve complete national liberation, and, internally, the elimination of the power and influence of the comprador class in the cities, the completion of the agrarian revolution in order to abolish feudal relations in the villages, and the overthrow of the government of the warlords."[4] It was essential to go through this kind of revolution before "a real foundation for the transition to socialism" could be laid.[5]

It is not difficult to see that in Mao's immediate strategy the target of the revolutionary movement was to be the big bourgeoisie in the urban areas and the feudal landlords and warlords whose base lay in the countryside. However, in a majority of his writings of the period Mao seems to have narrowed down his attention to the task of elimination only of the latter two classes by changing the agrarian relations in the countryside. The reason possibly was that the Chinese economy was predominantly rural and agrarian and, therefore, the elimination of the feudal classes looked more important for the success of the revolution.[6] As has been pointed out earlier, Mao himself believed that the Chinese economy of the period was only marginally capitalist and that the hold of the big bourgeoisie on the Chinese state was correspondingly small. It could therefore, in comparison, be ignored even if only for the moment.

This issue assumes some importance when we try to discover the reasons for Mao's belief that only violent revolution was most appropriate and most expected in Chinese conditions.

As we have seen in Chapter 1, Mao believed that the bourgeois parliamentary institutions could not be the instrument of the capture of power by the communists; these institutions could be used at best only to educate and prepare the workers for the inevitable revolutionary struggle which will take the form of a civil war. In other words, even in a bourgeois state the revolution will have to be ultimately violent. As we noted above, as per Mao's own analysis the Chinese state was primarily feudal. Further, even as a matter of historical fact the bourgeois parliamentary structures had not taken roots in China at the time when Mao carried out his above-mentioned analysis. In the middle of 1920s, in fact, they hardly existed in any respectable form.[7] Clearly, from Mao's point of view not only was a violent revolution inevitable in China, but even the scope for the peaceful preparation for an ultimately violent revolution did not exist here.

It is not surprising that under such a situation Mao justified the use of violent methods in the agrarian struggle right from the day one. Specifically, this justification rested on a two-fold belief: the Chinese peasantry was deeply resentful about the intense oppression it had had to bear under the existing relations, and the peasants had no option but to resort to violent methods given the deeply entrenched power of the feudal lords. As we shall see below, there was an additional tactical reason. Mao believed that the use of extreme violence in some cases will help the peasantry in psychologically overwhelming the feudal landlords.

As a matter of fact, the use of such methods was already being resorted to in the growing peasant movement in rural China. Specifically, this was happening in certain Kuomintang (KMT)-controlled areas in May 1927. In these areas, the peasants had organised themselves into associations and had started confiscating the land of the landlords under the direction of the peasant department of the Chinese Communist Party (CPC) then headed by Mao.[8]

Mao, who had stayed in the region between 1924 and 1926, and had toured it again in January-February 1927,[9] found the peasants arresting, humiliating and murdering those whom he called "local tyrants and evil gentry", looting their houses and killing their animals. "Doing whatever they like and turning everything upside down, they have created a kind of terror in the countryside", Mao noted approvingly. This was what some people called "going too far" or "exceeding the proper limits in righting a wrong" or "really too much". "Such talk may sound plausible", commented Mao, but in fact it was "wrong". Firstly, because "the lawless landlords" had "themselves driven the peasants to this". "For ages" they had "used their power to tyrannize…the peasants and trample them underfoot". That was why the peasants had "reacted so strongly". "The most violent revolts and the most serious disorders" had, according to Mao, "invariably occurred in places" where the landlords had "perpetrated the worst outrages". Secondly, "Without using the greatest force", the peasants could not "possibly overthrow the deeprooted authority of the landlords" which had "lasted for thousands of years".[10]

These, however, were not the only reasons for the use of violence against the rural gentry. According to Mao, there was a direct link between the use of violent methods and the strategic and tactical aims of the movement. Viewing the activities of the peasants in the light of these aims, he said: "There is a revolutionary significance in all the actions which were labelled as 'going too far' in this period". "It is necessary", he declared, "to create terror for a while in every rural area, or otherwise it would be impossible to suppress the…counter-revolutionaries in the countryside or overthrow the authority of the gentry". "Proper limits" had "to be exceeded in order to right a wrong", or else the wrong could not be righted.[11] Justifying execution in selected cases, Mao added: "The execution of one…big landlord reverberates through a whole county and is very effective in eradicating the remaining evils of feudalism. Every county has these major tyrants…and the only effective way of suppressing the reactionaries is to execute at least a few in each county who are guilty of the most heinous crimes". Citing instances of the frequent killings of the innocent people by the landlords, Mao asked: "…now that the peasants have risen and shot a few and created just a little terror in suppressing the counter-revolutionaries, is there any reason for saying they should not do so?"[12]

Standing People's Army

It can be seen from the above account that Mao's justification of the use of violence by peasants in the areas referred to above was largely post-facto. Secondly, although the peasants were being directed by the peasant department of the CPC, the confiscations and the killings were being carried out by the peasants themselves in a highly populistic manner. Although Mao's reasons for the justification of such violence did not change in the subsequent years, nevertheless certain developments that took place between 1926 and 1928 convinced him that the execution of violent tactics could no longer be left purely to the peasant initiative. On the contrary, the task of the perpetration of violence on the enemy classes must now be taken into the party hands and be performed in a more organised and systematic manner. The logical culmination of this line of thought was the insistence on the need of having a standing people's army, trained and used on regular military lines.

We noted above that Mao was initially in favour of suspending revolutionary hostility towards the national bourgeoisie. This was because of his belief that the latter had as yet an ambivalent attitude towards the workers' movement. Further, this attitude also stemmed at least partly from his view, which he shared with the Comintern, that the Chinese revolution was still at the bourgeois-democratic stage. This fact might make necessary an alliance with the national bourgeoisie against the other confirmed reactionary classes. It needs to be pointed out here that this alliance had actually materialised already in 1922 and was largely the handiwork of the Comintern.[13] However, by the end of 1927 the KMT, the political representative of the national bourgeoisie, had fallen out with the communists. It had, in fact, turned against them, and by the beginning of 1928 had virtually exterminated them.[14] This behaviour of the KMT was an alarmed response to the rapid growth and entrenchment of communist influence during the preceding years. These years had seen a strong workers' movement in the trail of the KMT advance. In certain areas, the movement had even preceded the march of the KMT army. This happened, for example, in Shanghai where the workers organised themselves into a militia and took control of the city. The leader of both these movements was the communist party.[15]

The sudden turn-about by the KMT evoked a sharp reaction from Mao and resulted in additional, in some ways totally new, theoretical insights about the political situation in China—insights which had far-reaching implications for the revolutionary strategy of the communist party. Mao expounded these insights in his article "Why is it that Red Political Power can Exist in China?" which he wrote in October 1928 while he was at the Chingkangshan plateau on the borders of Hunan and Kiangsi provinces. This was the area where Mao had established the first "Red" base after the first united front between the KMT and the CPC had collapsed.[16]

Analysing the internal political situation in China, Mao labelled the current KMT regime as "the new warlords of the Kuomintang". It was a regime "of the comprador class in the cities and the landlord class in the countryside". This regime had "capitulated to imperialism in its foreign relations" and had "replaced the old warlords with new ones, subjecting the working class and the peasantry to an even more ruthless economic exploitation and political oppression." The bourgeois-democratic revolution of 1926-27 "had gone only half way when the comprador and landlord classes usurped the leadership and immediately shifted it on to the road of counter-revolution". As a result, "throughout the country the workers, the peasants, the other sections of the common people, and even the [national] bourgeoisie"[17] "remained under counter-revolutionary rule". Mao believed that Chiang Kai-shek's was only one of the four "cliques of the new Kuomintang warlords", all of which were fighting bitterly among themselves. This struggle among the different cliques of warlords reflected "the contradictions and struggles among the imperialist powers".[18]

We can see that with the suppression of the communists by the KMT, the latter no longer represented, to Mao, the national bourgeoisie. Rather it had become an instrument of the comprador classes, namely the big bourgeoisie, the warlords and the feudal landlords. In terms of the nature of the state, this meant that after the capitulation of the KMT, the Chinese state had become all the more imperialist while still retaining its previous partly feudal character. Nevertheless, the economy continued to retain its partly capitalist nature, for, even though the national bourgeoisie no longer existed as a political force, its economic presence did not lose the space it occupied before. In terms of the goals of the revolutionary movement, these developments implied that the efforts to accomplish the tasks of the national bourgeoisie, namely, the emancipation of China from imperialism and the elimination of feudal relations in the countryside, now went neglected. The inevitable conclusion in terms of revolutionary strategy had to be that the struggle for the national bourgeois revolution would now have to be led by the proletariat itself. This is the conclusion Mao in fact arrived at after his examination of the national political scene in his above-mentioned article.[19] It is important to note in this connection that while Mao agreed with the Comintern and the central committee of the CPC that "the content of China's democratic revolution" consisted in "overthrowing the rule of imperialism and its warlord tools in China so as to eliminate the feudal exploitation of the peasants by the landlord class", he accused the CPC of having "failed to exercise firm leadership in the revolution of 1926-27, thereby allowing the comprador and landlord classes to seize the leadership and replace the revolution by counter-revolution."[20]

The facts that emerge from the preceding discussion are the following. Towards the end of 1928, the Chinese economy and state were almost totally dominated by the so-called comprador classes, namely, the warlords, the feudal landlords and the big bourgeoisie. These classes were not only better organised but also better armed than the proletariat, the class that in the complete absence of the national bourgeoisie as a political force had to lead the revolutionary struggle. Because of the very logic of the situation, this struggle had to be a national, bourgeois-democratic revolution. As we shall see below, it was these facts, alongwith a combination of certain other factors, that convinced Mao that violent armed struggle carried out on regular military basis was the only revolutionary strategy which would enable the revolutionary movement to defeat the opposing reactionary classes.

One of these factors mentioned above was the feasibility of "long-term survival inside" China "of one or more small areas under Red political power completely encircled by a white regime". This feasibility could not exist, believed Mao, in an imperialist country or in a colony under direct imperialist rule. It could exist only in a country like China which was not only economically backward but also semi-colonial and under indirect imperialist rule. It depended upon the existence of "another unusual phenomenon, namely war with the White regime". In the opinion of Mao, it was a feature of semi-colonial China that "ever since the first year of the Republic (1912)", the various cliques of the old and new warlords had "waged incessant wars against one another, supported by imperialism from abroad and by comprador and landlord classes at home".[21]

During the revolutionary struggle certain regions of China had already experienced the emergence of independent Red regimes through the use of armed struggle on military lines. This is how the independent regimes of peasants had come into existence "in Haifeng and Lufeng, in eastern and southern Hunan, in the Hunan-Kiangsi border area and in Huangan Hupeh Province".[22] This factor was complemented by another, namely that the current Red army was a split-off from the erstwhile National Revolutionary Army which had been involved in mass democratic struggles along with the workers and the peasantry and therefore did not lack democratic tradition.[23]

The presence of all these factors along with the conclusions he had reached through politico-economic analysis deepened Mao's conviction that conditions were ripe in China for the creation of a mass armed organisation on military lines. This organisation could be used, first, for the establishment of Red political bases in the countryside, and, then, for their expansion towards the urban centres.

In fact, Mao began to firmly believe that "the existence of a regular Red army of adequate strength" was "a necessary condition for the existence of Red political power" in China. If there were only local Red guards but no regular Red army, then the movement could not "cope with the regular white forces". Therefore, even when the masses of workers and peasants were active, it would be "definitely impossible" to create an independent regime which was "durable" and grew "daily", unless there were "regular forces of adequate strength". It followed that the idea of establishing independent regimes of the workers and peasants by armed force was "an important one which must be fully grasped by the Communist Party".[24]

In a report that he submitted to the central committee of the CPC just over a month later, Mao returned to this issue. "An independent regime", he repeated, "must be an armed one. Wherever such an area is located, it will be immediately occupied by the enemy if armed forces are lacking or inadequate..."[25] He recommended that the central committee "should devote great effort to military work".[26] One and a half years later, Mao was still hammering away at this theme. In the famous article "A Single Spark can Start a Prairie Fire", written in January 1930, he noted: "...in...China the establishment and expansion of the Red Army...and the Red Areas is the highest form of...struggle...and undoubtedly the most important factor in accelerating the revolutionary high tide throughout the country".[27]

It needs to be mentioned here that Mao wrote this sentence in the process of justifying his disagreement with the central committee of the CPC which believed that there was no need to establish Red political bases in China, an opinion which in turn implied the infructuousness of a regular and constantly expanding Red army. As reported by Mao, the committee was in favour of confining the military activity only to roving guerrilla actions till the masses had been readied to launch a countrywide armed insurrection in which the Red army, inevitably only in its guerrilla form, too would participate.

This opinion of the central committee led Mao to defend his thesis about the feasibility and necessity of Red political bases. According to him, the "theory that we must first win over the masses on a country-wide scale and in all regions and then establish political power does not accord with the actual state of the Chinese revolution". In Mao's view, this theory derived mainly from the failure to understand that China was a semi-colonial country over which many imperialist powers were contending. If one clearly understood this fact, only then could one understand why "the unusual phenomenon of prolonged and tangled warfare within the ruling classes" was "only to be found" in China, and why this warfare was steadily growing fiercer and spreading. This in turn would make one understand why the policy which merely called for roving guerrilla actions could not accomplish the task of accelerating the nation-wide revolutionary movement. What could accomplish it was the alternative policy "of establishing base areas; of systematically setting up political power; and...of expanding the people's armed forces by a comprehensive process of building up first the township Red Guards, then the district Red Guards, then the county Red Guards, the local Red Army troops, all the way up to the regular Red Army troops...etc."[28]

Regular Military War

We have seen so far that Mao's belief that a violent revolution was inevitable in China flowed from his analysis of the Chinese situation. Mao changed the conclusions of this analysis at least once, we saw, during the period from 1926 to 1930, bringing a corresponding change in his strategy of the revolutionary movement. Accordingly, the form of the violent struggle, too, did not remain similar in the two situations. Whereas in the earlier form it was the ordinary people and the people's militia who were to execute the violent tactics, in the later form this task was to be performed in a more organised and systematic manner by a regular military force.

However, the reader must have noticed that Mao had thus far discussed only the *need* for a standing military force; he had not clearly suggested the kind of struggle this force would wage. Would it be a regular military war, or only some form of civil war, which, needless to say, would be different from a regular war?

It is necessary to mention in this context that although Mao never clearly distinguished a civil war from a regular military war, which he also at times called a "national war", the distinction is implicit in his writings. We shall see below that the idea of revolution as a regular war emerged clearly after Mao's analysis of the Chinese situation in 1935 and later, an analysis the conclusions of which constituted, once again, a departure from his previous position.

The circumstances which prompted Mao to review his position was the occupation of Manchuria by Japan in 1931 and the probability that it would advance even further.[29] This brought three concrete and mutually related changes in Mao's positions: (1) at the level of the characterisation of the state, after the Japanese move China was no longer semi-colonial but rather a potential colony; (2) at the level of political strategy, the event had given rise to a need to form a united front with all nationalist forces, especially the national bourgeoisie, against Japanese imperialism; and (3) at the level of revolutionary strategy and tactics, it had created a situation in which the revolutionary struggle would have to be waged as a regular military war.

The main characteristic of the current situation in China, according to Mao, was that the "Japanese imperialism" wanted "to turn China into a colony".[30] This "basic change in the situation" had "changed the relationship among the various classes in China, strengthening the camp of national revolution and weakening that of counter-revolution".[31]

Elaborating this, Mao said that for nearly a hundred years, China had been a semi-colonial country jointly dominated by several imperialist powers. However, the people of China had always resisted and struggled against this imperialism. It was due to this struggle, and the conflicts among the imperialist powers, that China had been able to retain its semi-independent status. Despite this, Japan could annex exclusive domination over China for a time during the First World War. Japan's actions during the 1930s showed that this time its ambitions were greater. Now it wanted to physically occupy the whole of China and convert it from a semi-colony shared by several imperialist powers into a colony of Japan.[32]

From amongst the classes in China, the big bourgeoisie, the feudal landlords and the warlords, true to their comprador character, were helping Japan to realise its latest ambition in China. Since the interests of these classes were "inseparably linked with imperialism", they continued to believe that "revolution of whatever kind" was "worse than imperialism". Mao believed that "Japanese imperialism could not become so blatant in its aggression were it not for this pack of traitors". They were "the running dogs of imperialism", and therefore remained the "deadly enemies of the Chinese people" even in the new situation.[33]

Among the "people", Mao included the workers, the peasants and the petty-bourgeoisie, all of which according to him were in favour of resisting the Japanese imperialism. The workers and the peasants had been and still were, without any doubt, "the most resolute forces in the Chinese revolution". This was proved by their record in the revolution of 1924-27, the agrarian revolution from 1927 onwards, and the anti-Japanese movement since the occupation of Manchuria. As for the petty-bourgeoisie, the students and the urban sections of this class were already active in the anti-Japanese movement. The urban petty-bourgeoisie had also taken part in the revolution of 1924-27. Being small producers, their interests were irreconcilable with those of imperialism. Imperialism and the Chinese counter-revolutionary classes had caused them great harm, driving many of them into unemployment and bankruptcy. Faced with the immediate danger of becoming slaves to a foreign nation, they had no alternative but to resist the Japanese advance.[34]

Thus the positions of the counter-revolutionary and the revolutionary classes towards the impending Japanese colonialism were clear and unambiguous. In this respect, the only problematic class was the national bourgeoisie. Mao reiterated his previous view that this class had taken part in the revolution of 1924-27, but had later shown an ambivalent attitude towards the revolution. It had joined the reactionary classes, the leadership of which was then assumed by Chiang Kai-shek. At the same time, Mao asserted that under the new circumstances there was a possibility of certain sections of this class undergoing an attitudinal change. These were those sections which were less feudal and less comprador than the reactionary classes as they had fewer ties with the Chinese landed interests and with the foreign capital than the right wing of the national bourgeoisie. The possibility of attitudinal change was strengthened by the fact that during the years the national bourgeoisie had deserted the revolutionary camp, these sections had gained nothing except bankruptcy or semi-bankruptcy of their industrial enterprises. As to the extent of the change, it remained true that the general trait of the national bourgeoisie was to vacillate, but at a certain stage of the struggle the left wing of it might join progressive forces while the right wing might vacillate towards neutrality.[35]

Anticipating the likely objection that the Chinese national bourgeoisie could possibly not change its attitude because of its economic and political weakness, Mao contended that weakness could not be the reason for its inability. By that logic it should not have joined the revolution of 1924-27. The only thing that could possibly happen was that the comprador classes could try to entice it with the lure of some temporary advantage.[36]

On the basis of this analysis, Mao asserted that "when the national crisis reaches a crucial point, splits will occur in the Kuomintang camp".[37] These splits, which will be "unfavourable to the counter-revolution and favourable to the revolution",[38] would facilitate the task of forming "a broad revolutionary national united front", a front that was needed at the moment "to turn China into a free and independent country with full territorial integrity".[39]

Mao emphasised that it would not be possible for the front to realise this aim without waging a regular military war against Japan and its Chinese collaborators, a course of action that was not imperative earlier. In the earlier period imperialism was not making any direct armed attack on China. As a result, the communist party could fight against counter-revolution through the tactic of civil war alone. As examples Mao cited the party's struggles against the warlords jointly with the bourgeoisie in 1924-27, and the one against the warlords and the comprador bourgeoisie together with the peasants and the petty bourgeoisie after 1927. But now that imperialism had launched a direct armed attack on China, it was necessary for the party to unite all classes and strata in the country opposing Japan and wage a "national war" against it and its lackeys.[40]

In sum, then, Mao thought that a civil war against the comprador classes must be extended to become a regular military war when an imperialist power attempted to physically occupy the country with the open or tacit approval and help of these classes. It is clear that war, in its civil or regular military form, was the essential and the most central element in Mao's strategy of revolution in a semi-feudal, semi-colonial society that was in danger of becoming, partly or fully, a full-fledged colony. It would be appropriate to cite here certain views of Mao on war that he expressed in his writings over the years. These views would help us grasp better his understanding of war as an instrument of revolution, especially in China.

Asserting that "All wars everywhere in the world in which people rise up to fight their oppressors are just struggles",[41] Mao thought of war as "the highest form of struggle for resolving contradictions, when they have developed to a certain stage, between classes, nations, states, or political groups..." Such wars, however, have "different laws" directing them. These are "determined by the different circumstances of those wars...", including differences in their time and place. Hence the laws of one such war cannot be "mechanically applied" to another.[42] In the capitalist countries practising bourgeois-democracy, for example, the form of this war would be primarily civil war which would be preceded by a long legal and political struggle. In China, on the other hand, the situation was different. China was "not independent and democratic" but semi-colonial and semi-feudal, and was experiencing both feudal and imperialist oppression. The people here had "no parliament to make use of and no legal right" to peacefully organise themselves. Therefore, the task of the communist party here was "not to go through a long period of legal struggle before launching insurrection and war", but just the "reverse". Here, war was "the main form of struggle" and army "the main form of organisation". Other forms "such as mass organisation and mass struggle" were "also extremely important and indeed indispensable", and were "in no circumstances to be overlooked", but their purpose was "to serve the war". Mao quoted with approval, in this connection, Stalin's thesis that in China "the armed revolution" was "fighting the armed counter-revolution", and that this was "one of the specific features...of the Chinese revolution". Without armed struggle, therefore, the communist party "would have no standing at all in China, and it would be impossible to accomplish any revolutionary task". The CPC "did not grasp", according to Mao, "this point fully" during the twenties. "It did not then understand the supreme importance of armed struggle in China, or seriously prepare for war and organise armed forces, or apply itself to the study of military strategy and tactics". This was the reason why "the whole movement collapsed the moment the Kuomintang turned reactionary".[43]

Political Control over the Military

Such insistence by Mao on the use of armed struggle and war for establishing Red political power could give the impression that he over-emphasised the military means and neglected politics. As a matter of fact, however, throughout the period from 1926 to late 1930s covered above, he constantly warned against the dangers of, what he called, "the purely military viewpoint".[44] One reason for the defeat of the movement in the late 1927, according to him, was the policy of "adventurist advance"[45] that a section of the party had adopted at a time when "the masses…had not yet been aroused." Thus the insurrection had proved to be "pure adventurism".[46] Denouncing such a policy, Mao insisted on the use of "correct tactics", that is, "fighting no battle unless we can win it…"[47] He condemned those elements in the CPC which regarded "military affairs and politics as opposed to each other" and refused "to recognise that military affairs" were "only one means of accomplishing political tasks". These elements believed that "if you are not good militarily, you cannot be any good politically". This was tantamount, according to Mao, to giving "military affairs a leading position over politics". In reality, the Red army was only "an armed body for carrying out the political tasks of the revolution". It fought "not merely for the sake of fighting" but in order to help the masses "to establish revolutionary political power". Without this objective, fighting had no "meaning" and the Red army had no "reason for existence."[48]

Similarly, in the 1930s, while writing his famous sentence that "political power grows out of the barrel of a gun", Mao had added: "Our principle is that the Party commands the gun, and the gun must never be allowed to command the Party". This latter sentence has often been under-emphasised, even overlooked, while quoting the first, thus giving a false impression of Mao's strategy. Therefore, what Mao said immediately thereafter must be viewed in the light of the relationship established between politics and military in these two sentences. "All things grow out of the barrel of a gun" he wrote. "Experience in the class struggle in the era of imperialism teaches us that it is only by the power of the gun that working class and the labouring masses can defeat the armed bourgeoisie and the landlords; in this sense we may say that only with the gun can the whole world be transformed. We are the advocates of the abolition of war, we do not want war; but war can only be abolished through war, and in order to get rid of the gun it is necessary to take up the gun."[49]

This was in November 1938. Earlier, in his articles "Problems of Strategy in Guerrilla War Against Japan", and "On Protracted War", written in May-June 1938, Mao had expressed similar views. Regarding the relationship between politics and war particularly, he had written in the latter: "...war cannot for a single moment be separated from politics. Any tendency among the anti-Japanese armed forces to belittle politics by isolating war from it and advocating the idea of war as an absolute is wrong and should be corrected".[50]

Before we close this discussion of Mao's views on the use of the military means as an instrument of revolutionary struggle, we will present a brief exposition of how he thought the captured enemy soldiers, traitors and the ordinary Chinese helping enemy troops, etc., should be dealt with. This exposition will be a good illustration of the care and discrimination with which Mao always treated the question of the use of violence even during such an extremely violent process as a revolutionary war.

When in an interview on October 25, 1937, the British journalist James Bertram, questioned Mao's policy of giving lenient treatment to prisoners of war, Mao answered: "We will persevere in this policy of ours...We shall go on giving lenient treatment to captured Japanese soldiers and to those captured junior officers who have fought us under coercion; we shall not insult and abuse them, but shall set them free after explaining to them the identity of the interests of the people of the two countries. Those who do not go back may serve in the communist army".[51] Reiterating these views in May-June 1938, Mao underlined the importance of treating prisoners of war leniently. "The chief method of destroying them is to win over the Japanese soldiers politically", he wrote. "We should understand, rather than hurt, their pride and channel it in the proper direction", leading them "to see the anti-popular character of the aggression committed by the Japanese rulers".[52] Earlier, in the case of the KMT soldiers too Mao had advocated similar treatment for similar reasons. "The most effective method in propaganda directed at the enemy forces is to release captured soldiers and give the wounded medical treatment", he had written while still at the Chingkangshan mountain base. "Whenever soldiers, platoon leaders, or company, or battalion commanders of the enemy forces are captured...they are divided into those wishing to stay and those wishing to leave, and the latter are given travelling expenses and set free. This immediately knocks down the bottom out of the enemy's slander that 'the communist bandits kill everyone on sight'".[53] As for the Chinese who try "to sabotage, engage in disruption, stir up sedition or ferret out military secrets within the boundaries" of the communist-controlled region, they "may be arrested", and if convicted, "will be punished with due severity", but only upon "valid evidence".[54]

Tactical Use of Violence

We have so far elaborated Mao's views on the reasons for and the nature and the method of the application of violence in a revolution under semi-colonial, semi-feudal and partly bourgeois conditions. However, the reader must have noticed that our exposition has remained confined to the discussion of Mao's views on this subject only up to the stage of capture of power; it has not extended to the period when political power is already in the hands of the proletariat. We propose to explicate Mao's views on the status of violence at this stage of the revolution.

Before we proceed any further, however, we must draw the reader's attention to the fact that unlike in the case of Marx, Engels and Lenin, in Mao's conception of revolution during a certain phase of the revolution the stage of the dictatorship of the proletariat occurred simultaneously with the stage of the capture of power. Mao had to evolve this conception due to the peculiar situation in China where after a period certain territories had already fallen into the hands of the revolutionaries and therefore were ready for the administration of the dictatorship of the proletariat whereas the rest of the country was still to be captured. The concrete effect of this situation was that the tactics which were to be used against the formerly dominant classes in the areas under the rule of the proletariat were determined to some degree by the necessity of collaborating in the struggle for the capture of other areas with some of these same classes. In the Chinese revolution this phase continued right up to October 1949 when the national bourgeoisie was finally defeated. It is only after this date that the period of the dictatorship of the proletariat proper could be said to have begun, if at all.

We have seen above that Mao had insisted on the tactical use of violence. It needs to be noted here that this continued to be a characteristic of his policy throughout the remainder of his career, both before and after the final capture of power in 1949. In effect, this meant subtle shifts towards or away from moderation as the situation demanded, as we shall see below. As for the peculiar reason for these shifts, we have already noted it in the paragraph above.

Confiscation of Land and Industry

In March 1927, as we have seen, Mao had defended, and even advocated in certain cases, the murder of landlords and rural gentry on historical and moral grounds. But his opinion on this issue in these early years was more impetuous than considered. In later years, when the CPC was already in control of certain areas and was actually carrying out land reforms, Mao moderated his tone to some extent and, so far as the confiscation of land was concerned, even shifted his stand. Whereas earlier he had supported the forcible confiscation of all land, he now came to believe that the expropriation of land belonging to what he categorised "the intermediate class", that is, the class of "small landlords and rich peasants", was a mistake that stemmed from inexperience in the agrarian struggle. In 1929, the relevant provision in the Land Law promulgated in the Hunan-Kiangsi border area was changed from "confiscate all the land" to "confiscate the public land and the land of the landlord class". The aim of this change was to win over the intermediate class to the side of the small and poor peasants.[55] During the late 1930s when the anti-Japanese front was to be formed and it was found necessary to collaborate with the Kuomintang, the policy of forcible confiscation of land was totally abandoned, and the CPC became willing "to solve the land problem by legislative and other appropriate means in the course of building the new democratic republic". "The first question to be settled", according to Mao, was "whether China's land will be owned by the Japanese or by the Chinese".[56]

These shifts in the policy of land reforms, thrice within the period of approximately a decade, show Mao's extreme flexibility on the question of the use of violence. They make it clear that in spite of his belief in the necessity of a violent revolution in Chinese conditions, he paid close attention to the constantly changing situation and modified his approach in accordance with each new stage, depending upon whether the use of violence was advantageous or otherwise at a given stage.

During the early forties, Mao made a further shift towards moderation. He now proposed to accommodate the interests of the landlords to a considerable extent. They were now required only to reduce the rent and interest which they charged from the peasants. The peasants, on the other hand, were asked to pay this reduced rent and interests.[57] Similarly, in industry the "policy of suitably improving the workers' livelihood and of not hampering the development of the capitalist economy" was adopted. Mao characterised this as "the dual policy". As he put it: "In the sphere of political rights, it is the dual policy of allowing all the anti-Japanese landlords and capitalists the same rights of person...and property...as the workers and peasants and yet of guarding against possible counter-revolutionary activity on their part". This, according to him, was "the most revolutionary policy for China" of the day, and "to oppose or impede its execution" was "undoubtedly a mistake".[58]

After the compulsions of the period of the war against Japan had ended, Mao made a reversal in his land policy and did away with the concessions that had been granted to the big landlords.[59] But his attitude towards the intermediate class underwent no perceptible change. "When solving the land problem", he exhorted the party in 1946, "we should distinguish the ordinary rich peasants and middle and small landlords from the traitors, bad gentry and local tyrants". He asked the party to be "more strict" with the latter and "more lenient" towards the former.[60] As for the middle peasants, it was "absolutely impermissible to encroach on" their interests. If cases were to occur "where the interests of the middle peasants are encroached upon, there must be compensation and apology".[61] Similarly, "adventurist policies towards middle and small industrialists and merchants" were to be avoided. The "only industrial holdings" that were to be confiscated were those of "bureaucrat-capitalists and of real counter-revolutionary local tyrants." Thus, only "the handful of arch-criminals" who were "really guilty of the most heinous crimes" were "to be handed over to the people's courts to be tried and punished". And after the sentences had been "approved by the appropriate government organisations", it was "entirely necessary for the sake of revolutionary order to shoot them and announce their executions". This, however, was only "one side of the matter". The other side was that "we must insist on killing less and must strictly forbid killing without discrimination". To advocate killing more or killing without discrimination was "entirely wrong". It would cause the party "to forefeit sympathy, become alienated from the masses and fall into isolation". Therefore, the main emphasis should be on "saving" the landlords as individuals and on "remoulding" them. For, the task of the party was "to wipe out the landlords as a class, not as individuals".[62]

In the period that immediately followed, Mao repeatedly warned the party workers against indulging in the "ultra-left policy". In a speech to the cadres in April 1948, for example, he criticised the party organisation of the Shansi-Suiyan liberated area for failing "to adhere unequivocally to the Party's policy of strictly forbidding beating and killing without discrimination". The result of this failure of the party had been that some landlords and rich peasants had been "needlessly put to death" and "the bad elements" in the rural areas had been "able to exploit the situation".[63] To avoid such occurrences, according to Mao, the "system of feudal exploitation must be abolished step by step, that is, in a tactical way". And the tactics must be determined "according to the circumstances and the degree to which the...masses are awakened and organised".[64]

Mao's repeated stress on "discrimination" illustrates a substantial shift from the position in the late 1920s when he had justified the peasants' action in "going too far" and "exceeding the proper limits" while dealing with the landlords. We may note that Mao's stand in this particular matter was much softer than that of Lenin at the comparable stage of revolution. (Marx and Engels had not gone into the matter in such detail.) The difference obviously stems from their different conceptions of revolution. In the new democratic revolution which involved a considerable accommodation of the interests of certain upper classes till a particular time, Mao perhaps could not afford to be as harsh as Lenin could in his 'purer' 'socialist' revolution.

Suppression of the Reactionaries

Three months before the proclamation of the republic, in an article written on June 30, 1949, in commemoration of the twenty-eighth anniversary of the CPC, Mao had defined the precise nature of the new state as "the people's democratic dictatorship", which meant in effect "democracy for the people and dictatorship over the reactionaries".[65] But who were the people, and who the reactionaries? In 1949, as per Mao's definition, the people were "the working class, the peasantry, the petty-bourgeoisie and the national bourgeoisie", and the reactionaries were "the landlord class and the bureaucrat-bourgeoisie". In the new state, the people were to "enjoy the rights of freedom of speech, assembly, association and so on", and the reactionaries were to be "suppressed". In some cases, however, the policy of suppression was to extend to the people as well. These would be the cases where people broke law. In such cases, they too could be "imprisoned or even sentenced to death".

But this would differ "in principle from the dictatorship exercised over the reactionaries as a class". Overall, the method to be employed towards the people would be that of "persuasion", and not of "compulsion". Further, those members of even the reactionary classes who "do not rebel, sabotage or create trouble", and who show a willingness to "remould themselves through labour" would not be unduly punished.[66]

This policy was put into effect in 1951-52, first, in the campaign against the "counter-revolutionaries", and, later, in the "thought reform" movement and the campaigns against "three evils" and "five evils". These latter two campaigns were directed against the corrupt party officials and against those members of the national bourgeoisie who cheated and/or sabotaged against the state, respectively.[67]

In the case of counter-revolutionaries, Mao asked the party to "strike surely, accurately and relentlessly". He insisted on a "strict examination of the lists of persons to be arrested or executed". The number of persons to be killed, he said, "must be kept within certain proportions". Wrong executions should be avoided, but all those who deserved the death penalty must be eliminated. These would be the persons who owed "blood-debts" or "whose death is demanded by the people". Those whose crimes did not warrant death penalty should be "sentenced to…various prison terms or put under public surveillance".[68] As for party officials and members of the national bourgeoisie, for minor offences the guilty, according to Mao, should only "be criticised and educated", but in major offences they should "be sentenced to prison terms (to be reformed through labour), and the worst among them be shot".[69] The intellectuals, however, were to be let off comparatively lightly. Since they belonged essentially to the people, in the thought reform they were merely to be "educated and convinced" that they had anti-people views. This was to be done through criticism and self-criticism which, according to Mao, was one of the "democratic methods".[70]

In spite of these detailed instructions by Mao, however, at least 800,000 people are said to have been executed, jailed and/or sent to labour camps during this period.[71] According to some estimates, the figure was as high as two million executions alone, which amounted to about 0.3 percent of the total population of China at that time.[72]

In later years, too, Mao continued to emphasise and defend this policy off and on. In an article, in May 1955, for example, he wrote: "...in an era in which classes and class struggle still exist both at home and abroad, the working class and the masses who have seized state power must suppress the resistance to the revolution put up by all counter-revolutionary classes, groups and individuals, thwart their activities aimed at restoration and prohibit them from exploiting freedom of speech for counter-revolutionary purposes".[73] Similarly, in a conference in January 1962 he declared: "During the whole socialist stage there still exist classes and class struggle, and this...struggle is protracted, complex, sometimes even violent affair. Our instruments of dictatorship should not be weakened; on the contrary they should be strengthened".[74] In this speech, Mao also urged the party to adopt a "helpful attitude towards those who have made mistakes". "If people sincerely carry out self-criticism and are willing to correct mistakes", then they should be "forgiven".[75] This latter policy was to apply especially to the party and government officials, and it extended well into the period of the Cultural Revolution. Chiding the central committee of the CPC in April 1969, Mao said: "There are some places where too many people have been arrested. This is bad. Why arrest so many? They haven't committed homicide, arson, or poisoning?"[76] He asked the central committee to make precise distinctions among those who had "done bad things". Those who are frank should be treated leniently. Those who resist should be dealt with severely. And those who make a proper self-criticism should be allowed to keep working—but not in the positions of leadership.[77]

As can be seen, in his capacity as the leader of the newly established state Mao did not add much that was new to his old policy towards the classes and groups mentioned above. If at all, he seemed to have become more careful, discriminating and circumspect than before. Another remark that can be made with a degree of certainty is that our exploration of the pronouncements of Mao till 1969 does not throw up much evidence that Mao personally was in favour of unleashing indiscriminate mass terror against any section of the populace, including the reactionaries.

Cautious Approach

Mao's policy towards minority nationalities also proves the same point. Laying down this policy in June 1950, he declared:

> It is of vital importance to unite with the minority nationalities... Social reforms in their areas are a matter of great importance and must be handled cautiously. On no account must we be impetuous, for impatience will lead to trouble. No reform is to be instituted unless the conditions are ripe. Neither should any major reform be introduced where only one of the conditions is ripe...Of course, this is not to say that no reform at all is to be carried out...But the minority nationalities themselves must do the reforming.[78]

Specifically in the case of Tibet, Mao emphasised these views two years later. In a directive to the Southwest Bureau and the Working Committee of the CPC in Tibet (April 1952), he said: "We must do our best and take proper steps to win over the Dalai and the majority of his top echelon and to isolate the handful of bad elements in order to achieve a gradual, bloodless transformation of the Tibetan economic and political system over a number of years…" At the same time, he asked the Bureau to "be prepared for the eventuality of the bad elements leading the Tibetan troops in rebellion, and attacking" the communists, "so that in this contingency, the communist army could still carry on and hold out in Tibet."[79]

These two inner-party statements show Mao to be adopting a cautious approach so far as the task of carrying out reforms in the areas dominated by minority nationalities was concerned. He obviously preferred a peaceful transition, although he was not averse to using the force of arms when it was made inevitable.

Both these methods were amply used as the example of Tibet demonstrated. The Chinese army moved into Tibet on October 7, 1950 and occupied it, but only after nearly a year of propaganda to the effect that Tibet *will* be "liberated" and "reintegrated" into China, unilaterally if necessary. Later, on May 27, 1951, the Tibetan government was forced to sign an agreement with the Chinese government, ironically titled: "Agreement Between the Central People's Government and the Local Government of Tibet on Measures for the Peaceful Liberation of Tibet".[80] In accordance with this agreement, Tibet accepted the suzerainty of China over its territory. However, it was granted "national regional autonomy". Further, the status, power and functions of the Dalai Lama in the domestic context were not disturbed. In addition, it was laid down that the religious beliefs, habits and customs of the Tibetan people would be respected and their language promoted. As for reforms, they were to be carried out by the local government of Tibet "of its own accord", and no compulsion on the part of the central authorities in this regard was to be exercised.[81]

In the subsequent years, the Chinese governments repeatedly violated the provisions of this agreement in order to quicken the pace of reforms. But when it encountered resistance, it adopted a more conciliatory approach, at least for the time being.[82] The following statement of Mao reflects this change. In his speech to the Eleventh Session of the Supreme State Conference, on February 27, 1957, he said:

> Democratic reforms have not yet been carried out in Tibet, because conditions are not ripe…According to the seventeen-article agreement…the reform of the social system must be carried out, but the timing can only be decided when the great majority of the people of Tibet and the local leading public figures consider it opportune, and one should not be impatient.[83]

This moderation on the part of Mao, however, could not bear fruit because in March 1959, the Tibetan government and national assembly repudiated the 1951 agreement and proclaimed Tibet an independent and sovereign nation. The insurrection in and around Lhasa that preceded and continued after this proclamation was militarily suppressed by the Chinese government. A consequence of the uprising and its suppression was that the reforms that were so far being cautiously handled were now rapidly and intensively carried out.[84]

NOTES

[1] Mao, "Analysis of the Classes in Chinese Society", *Selected Works of Mao Tse-tung*, Volume I, Foreign Languages Press, Peking, 1977, p. 13.

[2] Ibid., pp. 13-14.

[3] Ibid., p. 14.

[4] Mao, "The Struggle in the Chingkang Mountains", *Selected Works*, Volume I, ibid., p. 97. See also, "Why is it that Red Political Power Can Exist in China?", ibid., pp. 63-64.

[5] Mao, "The Struggle in the Chingkang Mountains", *Selected Works*, Volume I, ibid., p. 97.

[6] A brief look at the contemporary rural China will be relevant here. In the 1920s, the majority of the farming population in China consisted of tenants. The average size of a farm was just 3.31 acres. Although the average produce from this farm was sufficient to feed a medium-sized family, 50 percent of it was usually appropriated by the landlord. This meant that the tenants had to borrow money during the period between sowing and harvesting. And with the interest rate as high as 30 percent or more, most of the tenants found themselves in perpetual debt. In addition, they had to pay a number of taxes to the warlords, their rulers in most places, usually in advance. All this left the peasants, including the middle and small owners, increasingly impoverished. This can be seen from the fact that whereas in 1918 50 percent of them were owners and 30 percent tenants, by 1926-27 the percentages were 25 and 55 respectively. But these figures pertain to the whole of China. In certain provinces, especially in the south, the conditions were even worse. In Hunan, for example, the tenants comprised 80 percent of the total population. See Jerome Ch'en, *Mao and the Chinese Revolution*, Oxford University Press, London, 1967, p. 71.

[7] On the vicissitudes of these structures in China from 1910 onwards, see Keneth Scott Latourette, *The Chinese: Their History and Culture*, The Macmillan Company, New York, and Collier Macmillan Limited, London, 1972, pp. 321-32; and Wolfram Eberhard, *A History of China*, Routledge & Kegan Paul Ltd., London, 1960, pp. 300-14. For a detailed account of the constitutional and democratic movement in China, see Li Chien Nung, *The Political History of China*, 1840-1928, D. Van Nostrand Company Inc., Princeton, 1956, Chapter VI onwards.

[8] See Jerome Ch'en., op. cit., pp. 107-10.

[9] Ibid., pp. 98, 104 and 111.

[10] Mao, "Report on Investigation of the Peasant Movement in Hunan", *Selected Works*, Volume I, op. cit., pp. 28-29.

[11] Ibid., p. 29.

[12] Ibid., pp. 38-39. Mao urged for restraint in certain areas, however, such as "smashing idols". He feared that the landlords would take advantage of such acts and would incite the superstitious peasants against the communists. "If too much of an effort is made, arbitrarily and pre-maturely, to abolish these things", he said, "the local tyrants...will seize the pretext to put about such counter-revolutionary propaganda as...'the peasant association is blasphemous and is destroying religion'...for the purpose of undermining the peasant movement." Therefore, the correct policy for the communists in such matters should be: "Draw the bow without shooting, just indicate the motions". It should be left for the peasants themselves "to caste aside the idols, and pull down the temples..." It would be "wrong for anybody else to do it for them". Ibid., p. 46.

[13] See Stuart R. Schram, *The Thought of Mao Tse-tung*, Cambridge University Press, Cambridge, 1989, p. 31.

[14] Se Keneth Scott Latourette, op. cit., pp. 330-31.

[15] See Fernando Claudin, *The Communist Movement: From Comintern to Cominform*, Part One, Monthly Review Press, New York and London, 1975, pp. 271-73.

[16] See Han Suyin, *The Morning Deluge: Mao Tse-tung and the Chinese Revolution*, Volume I: 1893-1935, Panther Books, Herts, 1979, p. 106.

[17] Mao uses the term 'bourgeoisie' here to denote the national bourgeoisie. See note 1 to Mao's article "Why is it that Red Political Power can Exist in China?", in *Selected Works*, Volume I, op. cit., p. 70.

[18] Ibid., p. 63.

[19] Ibid., p. 64.

[20] Ibid.

[21] Ibid., pp. 64-65.

[22] Ibid., pp. 65-66.

[23] Ibid., p. 66.

[24] Ibid.

[25] Mao, "The Struggle in the Chingkang Mountains", *Selected Works*, Volume I, ibid., p. 80.

[26] Ibid., p. 99.

[27] Mao, "A Single Spark Can Start A Prairie Fire", *Selected Works*, Volume I, ibid., p. 118.

[28] Ibid., pp. 117-18.

[29] See C. P. FitzGerald, *Mao Tse-tung and China*, Penguin Books, Harmondsworth, 1977, pp. 46-53; and Stuart R. Schram, *Mao Tse-Tung*, Penguin Books, Harmondsworth, 1977, pp. 192-203.

[30] Mao, "On Tactics Against Japanese Imperialism", *Selected Works*, Volume I, op. cit., p. 153.

[31] Ibid., p. 159.

[32] Ibid., pp. 153-54.

[33] Ibid., p. 155.

[34] Ibid., p. 154.

[35] Ibid., pp. 155-56.

[36] Ibid., p. 157.

[37] Ibid.

[38] Ibid., p. 158.

[39] Ibid., p. 162.

[40] Mao, "Problems of War and Strategy", *Selected Works of Mao Tse-tung*, Volume II, Foreign Languages Press, Peking, 1977, p. 220.

[41] Mao, "On Tactics Against Japanese Imperialism", *Selected Works*, Volume I, op. cit., p. 170.

[42] Mao, "Problems of Strategy in China's Revolutionary War", *Selected Works*, Volume I, ibid., pp. 180-82.

[43] Mao, "Problems of War and Strategy", *Selected Works*, Volume II, op. cit., pp. 219-22.

[44] Mao, "On Correcting Mistaken Ideas in the Party", *Selected Works*, Volume I, op. cit., p. 105.

[45] Mao, "Why is it that Red Political Power Can Exist in China?", *Selected Works*, Volume I, ibid., p. 68.

[46] Mao, "The Struggle in the Chingkang Mountains", *Selected Works*, Volume I, ibid., p. 78.

[47] Ibid., p. 101.

[48] Mao, "On Correcting Mistaken Ideas in the Party", *Selected Works*, Volume I, ibid., p. 106.

[49] Mao, "Problems of War and Strategy", *Selected Works*, Volume II, op. cit., pp. 224-25.

[50] Mao, "On Protracted War", *Selected Works*, Volume II, ibid., p. 153.

[51] Mao, "Interview with the British Journalist James Bertram", *Selected Works*, Volume II, ibid., p. 55.

[52] Mao, "On Protracted War", *Selected Works*, Volume II, ibid., p.177.

[53] Mao, "The Struggle in the Chingkang Mountains", *Selected Works*, Volume I, op. cit., pp. 85-86.

[54] Mao, "Proclamation by the Government of the Shensi-Kansu-Ningsia Border Region and the Rear Headquarters of the Eighth Route Army", *Selected Works*, Volume II, op. cit., p. 77.

[55] See, "The Struggle in the Chingkang Mountains", *Selected Works*, Volume I, op. cit., p. 87; and Notes 17 and 18 to this article in ibid., p. 104.

[56] Mao, "Tasks of the Chinese Communist Party", *Selected Works*, Volume I, ibid., p. 272.

[57] Mao, "Preface and Postscript to Rural Surveys", *Selected Works of Mao Tse-tung*, Volume III, Foreign Languages Press, Peking, 1977, p. 15.

[58] Ibid., pp. 14-15.

[59] See Note 4 to the article "A Three Months Summary", *Selected Works of Mao Tse-tung*, Volume IV, Foreign Languages Press, Peking, 1977, p. 118.

[60] Mao, "Smash Chiang Kai-shek's offensive by a War of Self-Defence", *Selected Works*, Volume IV, ibid., pp. 89-90.

[61] Mao, "Greet the New High Tide of the Chinese Revolution", *Selected Works*, Volume IV, ibid., p.124.

[62] Mao, "On Some Important Problems of the Party's Present Policy", *Selected Works*, Volume IV, ibid., pp. 183-86.

[63] Mao, "Speech at a Conference of Cadres in the Shansi-suiyan Liberated Area", *Selected Works*, Volume IV, ibid., p. 229.

[64] Ibid., p. 236.

[65] Mao, "On the People's Democratic Dictatorship", *Selected Works*, Volume IV, ibid., p. 418.

[66] Ibid., pp. 417-19.

[67] Han Suyin, *Wind in the Tower: Mao Tse-tung and the Chinese Revolution*, 1949-1975, Little, Brown and Company, Boston and Toronto, 1976, pp. 45-47; and Stuart R. Schram, *Mao Tse-tung*, op. cit., pp. 266-73.

[68] Mao, "Be Activists in Promoting the Revolution", *Selected Works of Mao Tse-tung*, Volume V, Foreign Languages Press, Peking, 1977, pp. 50-54.

[69] Ibid., p. 65.

[70] See Schram, *Mao Tse-tung*, op. cit., p. 268.

[71] See Han Suyin, *Wind in the Tower: Mao Tse-tung and the Chinese Revolution*, op. cit., p. 45.

[72] Schram, *Mao Tse-tung*, op. cit., p. 267. See also, Delia Davin, *Mao: A Very Short Introduction*, Oxford University Press, Oxford, 2013, p. 55.

[73] Mao, "In Refutation of Uniformity of Public Opinion", *Selected Works*, Volume V, op. cit., p. 172.

[74] Mao, "Talk at an Enlarged Central Work Conference", in *Mao Tse-tung Unrehearsed: Talks and Letters, 1956-71*, ed. Stuart R. Schram, Penguin Books, Harmondsworth, 1975, p. 168.

[75] Ibid., pp. 185-86.

[76] Mao , "Talk at the First Plenum of the Ninth Central Committee of the Chinese Communist Party", in Schram, ibid., p. 284.

[77] Ibid.

[78] Mao "Don't Hit Out in All Directions", *Selected Works*, Volume V, op. cit., p. 35.

[79] Mao, "On the Policies for Our Work in Tibet—Directive of the Central Committee of the Communist Party of China", *Selected Works*, Volume V, ibid., p. 74.

[80] See George Ginsburgs and Michael Mathos, *Communist China and Tibet: The First Dozen Years*, Martinuss Nijhoff, The Hague, 1964, pp. 7-10. See also, Note 1 to Mao's article mentioned at endnote 79 above.

[81] Ginsburgs and Mathos, ibid., pp. 14-15. For the text of the agreement, see *Tibet and the Chinese People's Republic: A Report of the International Commission of Jurists by its Legal Inquiry Committee on Tibet*, International Commission of Jurists, Geneva, 1960, pp. 215-18.

[82] See, *Tibet and the Chinese People's Republic: A Report*, ibid., pp. 167-76 and 180-81; and Tenzin Phuntsok, "Sino-Indian Interaction on Question of Tibet", unpublished M. Phil dissertation, Panjab University, Chandigarh, 1981, Chapter III.

[83] Mao, "On Correct Handling of Contradictions Among the People", *Selected Works*, Volume V, op. cit., p. 406.

[84] See Tenzin Phuntsok, op. cit., Chapter IV; and Ginsburgs and Mathos, op. cit., Chapters III and IV.

5

Conclusion

Since we have been summarising and interlinking our findings in each successive chapter, we will make only those observations here which could not have been made during the course of this study.

Loose and Disjointed

The status of violence in the Marxist theory of revolution has not been very systematically and, we may even say, consciously worked out. As a result, the Marxist concept of violence is extremely loose and disjointed. Firstly, the concept differs in significant details in the case of each successive thinker under discussion even though due to reasons we need not go into here we have treated the ideas of Marx and Engels as a single body of thought. Secondly, even within the thought of each particular thinker, shifts and stances exist which can be reconciled with his general view on violence only with great difficulty. As the reader should have noticed, this is particularly true of Marx-Engels and Lenin.

This entire study, from Chapters 1 to 4, substantiates the first point. As substantiation of the second point, we will briefly present the evidence here.

We have seen in Chapter 1 that Marx and Engels had argued, on the one hand, that a violent socialist revolution was inevitable and that this inevitability inhered in the very structures of the capitalist society as it historically developed. In the same chapter, we outlined the brief and specific alternate view that at places where bourgeois-democratic institutions had emerged and had become entrenched, the revolution need not necessarily be violent; on the contrary, it was more likely to be peaceful. We have already indicated that this view conflicts in a major way with the general theoretical argument referred to above. The realisation that democratic institutions could emerge and function over and above capitalist economic structures is entirely missing from the general argument. This realisation existed simultaneously but separately and was not elaborated in any significant detail, nor was any attempt made to reconcile it with the general argument by introducing in a systematic manner the necessary amendments. The argument in amended form would have clearly suggested that a violent socialist revolution is not necessarily inherent in bourgeois structures. But since such an amendment was never made, even in their later writings, despite the situation-specific belief about the possibility of a peaceful revolution, we continue to find the assertion that the transformation of a capitalist society into a socialist one was bound to be violent.

Further, the order and coherence apparent in Marx's and Engels' argument as presented in the second chapter is really ours. In their own political writings on the likely nature of revolution on the continental Europe, they barely suggest this argument. Moreover, their view, systematised by us, that the revolution on the continent would be violent because of the inadequate development of the bourgeois-democratic institutions remains un-reconciled with their general view on violence elaborated primarily in *The Communist Manifesto* and later in the *Capital.*

When we come to Lenin, we find him arguing, like Marx and Engels in the case of continental Europe, that the violent nature of the socialist revolution in Russia was determined by the authoritarian/ autocratic political institutions. Like Marx and Engels, again, he ascribed this nature of these institutions to their late or obstructed development over capitalist economic structures which had already become predominant. As we have pointed out in Chapter 3, it should logically follow from this that once bourgeois political institutions had emerged over capitalist economic structures, it would become possible to make a peaceful revolution. But Lenin refused to reach this logical culmination and insisted instead that the revolution would remain violent under all circumstances. This was so because even the bourgeois state, according to him, remained authoritarian by virtue of being the monopoly of a particular class. We will not question here this particular belief of Lenin. It serves our purpose if we merely point out that this belief is not compatible with his argument of a violent revolution being engendered by the late or obstructed development of bourgeois political institutions. Further, this belief also conflicts with his argument, extended in *The State and Revolution* and presented in Chapter 1 here, that in England and America a peaceful revolution was perhaps possible in 1870s but was no longer so in 1917 when the participation of these countries in the imperialist war had bureaucratised and militarised their political institutions. Seen in conjunction with his belief that the imperialist war made a civil war inevitable, this argument of Lenin clearly leads to the conclusion that a violent revolution is not inevitably inherent in bourgeois political institutions—a conclusion that runs counter to his view of these institutions.

As for Mao, he argues convincingly that the revolution in a semi-feudal and semi-colonial country like China would be violent because of the deep-rooted economic and political entrenchment of the feudal class on the one hand and the presence of the colonial powers on the other. But his additional assertion that the bourgeois parliamentary institutions will not facilitate a peaceful attempt at revolution remains nothing more than an assertion. His own evidence or argument in support of this is almost non-existent. This assertion rests merely on his unsubstantiated and unelaborated view that no ruling class would give up its power without a violent struggle.

Four Strands

Initially, I intended to discuss here the current relevance of the Marxist concept of violence as it developed from Marx up to Mao. But as we have shown in the previous pages, a coherent and comprehensively discussed Marxist concept of violence is practically non-existent. Nevertheless, at a simplified level, four strands of this concept can be separated and discussed.

Causal Connection

At one level, it has been argued that the very nature of the bourgeois economic and political structures and institutions makes a violent socialist revolution inevitable. The exploitative bourgeois economic structures, it has been contended, have the invariable tendency to develop authoritarian political institutions over them. The characteristic authoritarianism of these institutions, which remain the monopoly of the bourgeois class, and the resultant oppressive political conditions for the subordinate classes, make it impossible for the working class to resort to peaceful methods of bringing desirable change in their situation.

Our exposition in Chapter 1 makes it clear that the argument on which this proposition is based assumes a causal connection between the economic structures on the one hand and political institutions on the other. That is, if the economic structures are exploitative, then the political institutions are bound to be oppressive. Secondly, it explicitly believes that this nature of these structures and institutions will continue to remain unchanged, and if at all there is a change, it will be in the negative direction. It is these assumptions and beliefs that lead to the conclusion that the working class will, and should, respond by making a violent revolution.

There is a view, however, that this need not always be the response of the workers. Karl Popper has suggested that the workers may not go in for a violent revolution because they may not acquire class consciousness or achieve class solidarity in the first place. The acquisition of this consciousness and solidarity may get blocked by the growing improvement in the material conditions of the workers on the one hand and the divisions among the different strata of their class that may emerge with the development of capitalism on the other.[1]

We need not subscribe fully to this view of Popper because the improvement in the material conditions of the workers may not take place without the struggle waged by them for this very purpose. This struggle will presuppose the existence of class consciousness and class solidarity among the workers although this consciousness may stay at the level of trade union consciousness, in the sense in which Lenin has used these words.

Therefore, the more important point is that the workers may not resort to violent methods of bringing change even after having acquired class consciousness and achieved class solidarity. This could happen in a place where the exploitation inherent in the economic structures has been mitigated through the workers' pressure upon the political structures. The workers at such a place may become more interested in the further improvement of their conditions *within* the system through greater pressure, and possible participation. And this may continue till the political structures allow this. Only after the political structures have become inflexibly rigid and totally unresponsive are the workers likely to think in terms of resorting to violent methods.

This eventuality, however, may not come about. For, it may become difficult, even impossible, for the ruling classes to block the further democratisation of the political structures, values and traditions once they have taken root in a given society and therefore the demands of the workers may gradually get accommodated to an unspecifiable extent. If this happens, a violent socialist revolution may get indefinitely postponed.[2]

If the above argument were to be accepted as correct, it would mean that there may not be a direct causal relationship between the nature of the economic and the political structures in the sense in which the economic structures are basic and therefore shape the nature of the political structures in their own mould. As per this implication, democratic political structures may arise over exploitative economic structures and may themselves be instrumental in making the economic structures less exploitative. The causal relationship, if there is one, that is, may in fact work in the reverse direction.

Two Defects

At the second level, the comparatively brief and specific alternate proposition says that the revolution may take a peaceful turn at places where bourgeois-democratic political institutions have emerged and become entrenched. It is clear from Marx's statements that according to him the working class would be able to make a peaceful revolution because the workers form the majority of the population. Being in majority, they would be able to capture power through universal suffrage and using this power would peacefully but rapidly transform the bourgeois structures into socialistic ones. This scenario, however, has two defects.

Firstly, the working class need not necessarily form the majority of a bourgeois-democratic society. And further development of capitalism may decrease, rather than increasing, the numbers of the working class by pushing more and more of the workers into the middle classes.[3] Now, if the working class may not form the majority, or if its numerical strength goes on progressively decreasing because of the tendency of the middle classes to increase, then it may have to compromise with and take along certain sections of the middle classes in order to come into power through universal suffrage. This will compel the working class to moderate its programme of rapidly transforming the system after coming into power, because in this eventuality the working class will not be the only class that will be holding the levers of power, and therefore will not be free to act according to its wishes. As was pointed out by Eduard Bernstein more than a hundred years ago: "In a democracy the parties, and the classes standing behind them, soon learn to know the limits of their power, and to undertake each time only as much as they can reasonably hope to carry through under the existing circumstances...The right to vote in a democracy makes its members virtually partners in the community, and this virtual partnership must in the end lead to real partnership".[4] That this indeed was happening in the case of working class parties in western Europe, especially in Germany, in the second half of the nineteenth century was shown by Bernstein.[5]

In the twentieth century, the continuation of this development was noted, among others, by Ralph Miliband: "In the twentieth century this trend has...come to dominate large (and in some cases the largest) working-class parties in capitalist countries. Britain, Germany and Sweden are obvious instances". Miliband observed that even though these parties cannot be said to have abandoned their commitment to the achievement of socialism, nevertheless, "it must be obvious that the parties concerned are in fact parties of social reform, whose leaders and leading personnel are in their overwhelming majority solidly and comfortably established in the existing social order, and who have absolutely no intention of embarking on anything resembling its wholesale transformation...Their purpose is reform, very often conceived in more or less the same way as it is by their conservative counterparts, as a necessary insurance against pressure for reforms of a too radical and rapid kind".[6] The failure to realise fully the possibility of these developments, or, in any case, to pay sufficient attention to their contemporary emergence forms the second defect in the scenario of a peaceful revolution presented by Marx and Engels.

Firmly Grounded

At the third level, the argument follows from the previous two streams. Citing the example of continental Europe (Marx and Engels) and tsarist Russia (Lenin), it has been suggested that at places where bourgeois economic structures have emerged and have become generally predominant but the development of bourgeois-democratic institutions is partial or has been totally obstructed, the revolution will inevitably adopt a violent form.

It should be clear that in this suggestion the arguments about the inevitability of a violent revolution under authoritarian political structures and the possibility of a peaceful revolution under bourgeois-democratic institutions have both been incorporated. Nevertheless, the suggestion veers off the earlier two arguments in one respect: it indicates that it is the continuing existence of precapitalist and therefore authoritarian political institutions over predominantly bourgeois economic structures that makes a violent socialist revolution inevitable. And, empirically it is this suggestion that seems to have been most firmly grounded. For, historically violent socialist revolutions have taken place not under bourgeois political institutions but all of them invariably in precapitalist, authoritarian states—states in which, nevertheless, bourgeois economic structures had at least partially taken root. Therefore, accepting the fact that under developed capitalism both the main components of the Marxist concept of violence have taken historical beating, it is the above-mentioned suggestion that should be made the basis for speculation on the likely nature of revolution in societies where bourgeois economic structures have emerged and have struck root but the nature and/or functioning of the political institutions still remains dominantly precapitalist and authoritarian.

Despite the 'collapse' of communism towards the later decades of the twentieth century and the then fashionable 'end of history' theory, which has still not fully lost its popular currency, in none of such societies the possibility of a violent socialist or at least socialistically oriented revolution can be totally or permanently ruled out. Nevertheless, this possibility seems to be far less now than 100-150 year ago when the capitalist system was neither so pervasive nor had it demonstrated its potential so successfully. This pervasiveness and demonstrated potential of the capitalist system could, in these societies, create movements for (greater) democracy through reform of political institutions while retaining the existing capitalist economic structures, instead of movements that would lead to a violent socialist transformation.

Such movements, if they turn out to be even partially successful, would transform these societies into societies where bourgeois-democratic institutions are getting slowly established. And if in the longer run they too come to achieve the same degree of development of democratic institutions as found in the developed capitalist societies, then the Marxist theory of violent revolution would likely meet the same fate here as it met in those societies.

Nevertheless, there is a need to point out here the connection between the development and entrenchment of democratic institutions and the late entry/emergence of capitalism in such societies. Because of the late entry/emergence of capitalism and the consequent delay in modern economic development, there would be greater strain on the distributive capacity of the democratic institutions here. Specifically, this strain would be the result of the accumulation of certain socio-economic problems over the years and the concomitant increase in expectations from the political system. The strain would be particularly intense in societies with complex and historically deep-rooted socio-cultural divisions. Such strain could give rise to authoritarian tendencies within a particular society, leading to the reemergence or reimposition of authoritarian rule. The imposition of such rule would open up once again the possibility of a violent socialist revolution at some future date.

This disadvantage caused by the late entry/emergence of capitalism could be offset, however, by the higher stage at which technology, whether indigenously developed or imported, would be available to these societies as compared with the developed capitalist societies which had to develop this technology over a long period of time. It has been argued that it is technology coupled with democracy that has been the primary factor behind the present prosperity and comparative stability of the developed capitalist societies.[7]

This particular 'force of production', to use the Marxist terminology, instead of destroying the capitalist mode of production, may yet save, from the threat of a violent socialist revolution, the fledgling capitalism that is slowly getting entrenched in a number of societies.

Our argument in the above paragraphs has been based on the assumption, it should be clear, that the societies that we have been talking about would become 'developing democracies'. There is a view, however, that in spite of the presence of democratic political institutions, such societies remain basically authoritarian. This view is based on a differentiation between the concept of state on the one hand and government or regime on the other. State, in this view, refers to "the permanent institutions of government and the concomitant ensemble of class relations which have been embedded in these same institutions". The government refers to "those political officials who occupy the executive and legislative positions and are subject to renewal or replacement". The author of this view, James Petras, contended that democratisation did not change the nature of the state but only led to changes at the level of the government or regime. "The new political regime exercises its prerogatives, executive and legislative initiatives within the framework established by pre-existing configuration of power".[8]

The implication of this view in the present context is clear: since democratisation does not change the basic nature of the state, developing democracies remain the site of a possible future violent socialist revolution.

From the empirical evidence presented by Petras it does indeed appear that developing democracies retain a large number of authoritarian elements. However, unlike Petras, in the context of the so-called bourgeois democracies, Marx and Engels do not make a distinction between the state and the government or regime. It is clear from their remarks that the existence and operation of bourgeois-democratic institutions and practices signify a reduction in the authoritarian character of the state to that degree, thereby correspondingly increasing the possibility of a peaceful socialist transformation.

Neo-imperialism

Petras has, however, Lenin and Mao as company both of whom largely rejected the above-mentioned view of Marx and Engels. This rejection was premised, particularly in the case of Lenin, on their reading of bourgeois imperialism as a force that played a major role in shaping the nature of states both at the centre and at the periphery. As we have seen in Chapter 3, for Lenin, during the period of imperialist war particularly, the bourgeois-democratic states engaged in war got bureaucratised and militarised, thus losing the democratic content, if any, that they had. Similarly, Mao, in a different context, held the direct or indirect presence of imperialism partially responsible for the authoritarian nature of a semi-feudal, semi-bourgeois state at the periphery. It should be clear that at this the fourth level of discussion in the Marxist concept of violence the argument of Mao would be comparatively more relevant at a time when the world is not witnessing any imperialist war, especially at the centre. However, even the argument of Mao would lose much of its substance when the phenomenon of colonialism has demised. Nevertheless, if we treat 'neo-imperialism' as the manifestation of the 'indirect presence of imperialism', part of Mao's argument would continue to be relevant.

And it is here that a certain analysis of neo-imperialism by James Petras and Morris Morley assumes significance.[9] If we were to generalise their argument and project it into the future, an important reason for the authoritarianism of developing democracies would be the willingness of their regimes to let neo-imperialism dictate their economic policies. These neo-liberal policies may lead to economic decline and/or mass poverty, inequality and deep social polarisation. With the consequent breakdown of traditional political controls exercised by political parties and trade unions on the one hand and mass protests, street mobilisations and unauthorised strikes on the other, the democratic states may increasingly assume authoritarian shape. If this happens, they would become vulnerable to the emergence of a violent socialist revolution.

NOTES

[1] K. R. Popper, *The Open Society and Its Enemies*, Volume 2, Routledge & Kegan Paul, London and Henley, 1977, pp. 147-56. As a matter of fact, Marx himself pointed out the emergence of this development in the England of his time when he wrote, in 1850, that the Chartist movement was getting

divided into two factions. The faction which represented the "revolutionary... tendency" within Chartism was the "mass of the workers living in really proletarian conditions"; the other faction belonged to the "purely democratic tendency" and consisted of "labour aristocracy" and the petty bourgeoisie. (Marx, *The Revolutions of 1848: Political Writings*, Volume 1, Ed., David Fernbach, Penguin Books, London, 1973, p. 308.) Later, Lenin too acknowledged this stratification within the working class and labelled the "labour aristocracy", or "this stratum of workers-turned-bourgeoisie", as the "real vehicles of reformism" in the working class movement. (See, Pradhan H. Parasad, "Political Economy of India's Retarded Development", *Economic and Political Weekly*, Bombay, January 27, 1990.) The existence of this phenomenon in contemporary advanced capitalist societies was reemphasised by some ex-Marxist scholars. See, for example, Adam Przeworski, "Class, Production and Politics", cited by James Petras in his "Retreat of the Intellectuals", *Economic and Political Weekly*, Bombay, September 22, 1990. Petras found such an analysis problematic in a major way. According to him, it "conflates class formation with class consciousness", and by denying the latter, it denies the former. In the process, it blinds itself to a basic tenet of Marxist theory, namely that "the transformation of a class in itself to a class for itself required political organization, education and ideological debates". (Ibid.) We incorporate this argument of Petras into our analysis immediately below.

[2] Our argument in the preceding paragraphs is based largely on, but is not necessarily exactly similar to, C. Wright Mill's critical observations on the Marxian theory and the picture that he presented of the advanced capitalist socicties in his book *The Marxists*, Penguin Books, Harmondsworth, 1975, Chapter 6.

[3] Among the Marxists, Eduard Bernstein was perhaps the first to point out this development in 1890s. See Leszek Kolakowski, *Main Currents of Marxism*, Volume II, Clarendon Press, Oxford, 1978, p. 106.

[4] Eduard Bernstein, *Evolutionary Socialism*, Schocken Books, New York, 1961, p. 144.

[5] Ibid., pp. 135-36.

[6] Ralph Miliband, *Marxism and Politics*, Oxford University Press, Oxford, 1977, p. 157. See also, C. Wright Mills, op. cit.

[7] See, for example, Daniel Bell, *The Coming of Post-Industrial Society: A Venture in Social Forecasting*, Arnold-Heinemann Publishers (India) Private Limited, New Delhi, 1974.

[8] James Petras, "Retreat of the Intellectuals", op. cit.

[9] James Petras and Morris Morley, "Latin America: Poverty of Democracy and Democracy of Poverty", *Economic and Political Weekly*, Bombay, July 27, 1991.

Bibliography

Primary Sources

Books

Engels, Frederick. 1975. *Anti-Duhring.* Moscow: Progress Publishers.

Karl Marx: Selected Writings. 1977. Ed. David McLellan. Oxford: Oxford University Press.

Lenin, V. I. 1960-1970. *Collected Works*, Volumes 1-45. Moscow: People's Publishing House, and Progress Publishers.

--------. 1982. *On the Dictatorship of the Proletariat.* Moscow: Progress Publishers.

--------. 1981. *The Socialist Revolution.* Moscow: Progress Publishers.

Mao Tse-tung. 1977. *Selected Works of Mao Tse-tung*, Volumes I-V. Peking: Foreign Languages Press.

Mao Tse-tung Unrehearsed: Talks and Letters, 1966-71. 1975. Ed. Stuart R. Schram. Harmondsworth: Penguin Books.

Marx, Karl. 1977. *Capital*, Volume 1. Moscow: Progress Publishers.

--------. 1973. *Surveys from Exile: Political Writings*, Volume 2. Ed. David Fernbach. Harmondsworth: Penguin Books, and London: New Left Review.

--------. 1981. *The First International and After : Political Writings*, Volume 3. Ed. David Fernbach. Harmondsworth: Penguin Books, and London: New Left Review.

--------. 1975. *The Poverty of Philosophy.* Moscow: Progress Publishers.

--------. 1973. *The Revolutions of 1848: Political Writings*, Volume 1. Ed. David Fernbach. Harmondsworth: Penguin Books, and London: New Left Review.

Marx, Karl, and Frederick Engels. 1975. *Collected Works*, Volume 4. Moscow: Progress Publishers.

--------. 1977. *Collected Works*, Volume 7. Moscow: Progress Publishers.

--------. 1975. *Selected Correspondence*. Moscow: Progress Publishers.

--------. 1976. *Selected Works*, Volumes One to Three. Moscow: Progress Publishers.

--------. 1976. *The German Ideology*. Moscow: Progress Publishers.

--------. 1975. *The Holy Family*. Moscow: Progress Publishers.

--------. 1978. *The Socialist Revolution*. Moscow: Progress Publishers.

The Political Thought of Mao Tse-tung. 1969. Ed. Stuart R. Schram. Harmondsworth: Penguin Books.

Secondary Sources

Books

Avineri, Shlomo. 1977. *The Social and Political Thought of Karl Marx*. New Delhi: S. Chand and Company.

Bell, Daniel. 1974. *The Coming of Post-Industrial Society: A Venture in Social Forecasting*. New Delhi: Arnold-Heinemann Publications (India) Private Limited.

Bernstein, Eduard. 1961. *Evolutionary Socialism*. New York: Shocken Books.

Blackburn, Robin (ed.). 1977. *Revolution and Class Struggle: A Reader in Marxist Politics*. Glasgow: Fontana/Collins.

Braunthal, Julius. 1966. *History of the International, Volume 1, 1864-1914*. London: Thomas Nelson and Sons.

--------. 1967. *History of the International, Volume 2, 1914-1943*. London: Thomas Nelson and Sons.

Ch'en, Jerome. 1967. *Mao and the Chinese Revolution*. London: Oxford University Press.

Claudin, Fernando. 1975. *The Communist Movement: From Comintern to Cominform*, Part One. New York and London: Monthly Review Press.

Cliff, Tony. 1985. *All Power to the Soviets*. London: Bookmarks.

Cohen, Arthur A. 1964. *The Communism of Mao Tse-tung*. Chicago and London: The University of Chicago Press.

Cole, G. D. H. 1961. *Communism and Democracy, 1914-1931*. London: Macmillan and Co. Ltd.

--------. 1954. *Socialist Thought: Marxism and Anarchism, 1850-1890*. London: Macmillan & Co. Ltd.

--------. 1963. *The Second International, 1869-1914*, Part I. London: Macmillan.

Colletti, Lucio. 1978. *From Rousseau to Lenin: Studies in Ideology and Society*. New Delhi: Oxford University Press.

Conquest, Robert. 1976. *Lenin*. Glasgow: Fontana/Collins.

Crankshaw, Edward. 1976. *The Shadow of the Winter Palace: The Drift to Revolution*. London and Basingstoke: Macmillan London Limited.

Das, Saitya Brata and Soumyabrata Choudhury (eds.). 2015. *The Weight of Violence: Religion, Language, Politics*. New Delhi: Oxford University Press.

Davin, Delia. 2013. *Mao: A Very Short Introduction*. Oxford: Oxford University Press.

Eberhard, Wolfram. 1960. *A History of China*. London: Routledge & Kegan Paul Ltd.

FitzGerald, C. P. 1977. *Mao Tse-Tung and China*. Harmondsworth: Penguin Books.

Ginsburgs, George, and Michael Mathos. 1964. *Communist China and Tibet: The First Dozen Years.* The Hague: Martinuss Nijhoff.

Kochan, Lionel, and Richard Abraham. 1983. *The Making of Modern Russia.* Harmondsworth: Penguin Books.

Kolakowski, Leszek. 1978. *Main Currents of Marxism*, Volumes I and II. Oxford: Clarendon Press.

Latourette, Keneth Scott. 1972. *The Chinese: Their History and Culture.* New York: The Macmillan Company, and London: Collier Macmillan Limited.

Lenin: A Biography. 1983. Moscow: Progress Publishers.

Lichtheim, George. 1974. *Marxism: An Historical and Critical Study.* London: Routledge and Kegan Paul.

Mattick, Paul. 1978. *Anti-Bolshevik Communism.* London: Merlin Press.

McLellan, David. 1973. *Karl Marx: His Life and Thought.* London: The Macmillan Press.

--------. 1979. *Marxism After Marx: An Introduction.* London and Basingstoke: Macmillan.

Mehring, Franz. 1948. *Karl Marx: The Story of His Life.* London: George Allen and Unwin.

Miliband, Ralph. 1977. *Marxism and Politics.* Oxford: Oxford University Press.

Miller, Richard W. 1984. *Analyzing Marx: Morality, Power and History.* Princeton: Princeton University Press.

Mills, C. Wright. 1975. *The Marxists.* Harmondsworth: Penguin Books.

Nung, Li Chen. 1956. *The Political History of China*, 1840-1928. Princeton: D. Van Nostrand Company Inc.

Phuntsok, Tenzin. 1981. "Sino-Indian Interaction on Question of Tibet". Unpublished M. Phil dissertation. Chandigarh: Panjab University.

Popper, K. R. 1977. *The Open Society and Its Enemies*, Volume 2. London and Henley: Routledge and Kegan Paul.

Riazanov, David. 1973. *Karl Marx and Friederich Engels: An Introduction to Their Lives and Work*. New York and London: Monthly Review Press.

Ryan, James. 2014. *Lenin's Terror: The Ideological Origins of Early Soviet State Violence.* London and Abingdon: Routledge.

Schapiro, Leonard. 1960. *The Communist Party of Soviet Union.* London: Eyre and Spottiswoode.

Schram, Stuart R. 1989. *The Thought of Mao Tse-tung.* Cambridge: Cambridge University Press.

Singer, Peter. 2000. *Marx: A Very Short Introduction.* New York: Oxford University Press.

Smith, S. A. 2002. *The Russian Revolution: A Very Short Introduction.* New York: Oxford University Press.

Suyin, Han. 1979. *The Morning Deluge: Mao Tse-tung and the Chinese Revolution*, Volume I: 1893-1935. Herts: Panther Books.

--------. 1976. *Wind in the Tower: Mao Tse-tung and the Chinese Revolution*, 1949-1975. Boston and Tronto: Little, Brown and Company.

Tibet and the Chinese People's Republic: A Report of the International Commission of Jurists by its Legal Inquiry Committee on Tibet. 1960. Geneva: International Commission of Jurists.

Ulam, Adam B. 1977. *Lenin and the Bolsheviks.* Glasgow: Fontana/Collins.

Wolfe, Bertram D. 1948. *The Three Who Made a Revolution.* New York: The Dial Press.

Žižek, Slavoj. 2009. *Violence: Six Sideways Reflections.* London: Profile books.

Papers

Finlay, Christopher J. 2006. "Violence and Revolutionary Subjectivity: Marx to Žižek". UCD Geary Discussion Paper Series, January 11. http://www.ucd.ie/geary/static/publications/workingpapers/GearyWp200601.pdf

Johnston, Monty. 1983. "Marx, Blanqui and Majority Rule". In Ralph Miliband and John Saville (eds.), *The Socialist Register*, 1983. London: The Merlin Press.

Parsad, Pradhan H. 1990. "Political Economy of India's Retarded Development". Bombay: *Economic and Political Weekly*, January 27.

Petras, James. 1990. "Retreat of the Intellectuals". Bombay: *Economic and Political Weekly*, September 22.

Petras, James, and Morris Morley. 1991. "Latin America: Poverty of Democracy and Democracy of Poverty". Bombay: *Economic and Political Weekly*, July 27.

Wolfe, Bertram D. 1973. "Leninism". In Milorad M. Drachkovitch (ed.), *Marxism in the Modern World*. Stanford: Stanford University Press.

Index

About the Author

Rustam Singh holds M.Phil. (Gold Medal) and Ph.D. degrees in political science and political philosophy, respectively. He has held various research and editorial positions including the following: assistant editor of *Economic and Political Weekly*, Bombay; research associate at Centre for the Study of Developing Societies, Delhi; fellow at Indian Institute of Advanced Study, Shimla; editor of *Summerhill IIAS Review*, a journal of Indian Institute of Advanced Study, Shimla; founding editor (with Ashok Vajpeyi) of *Hindi: Language, Discourse, Writing*, a journal of Mahatama Gandhi International Hindi University; and visiting fellow at Centre for Philosophy, Jawaharlal Nehru University, New Delhi. He is currently a senior fellow and senior editor in the publications wing of Eklavya, an NGO active in Madhya Pradesh, India.

His essays and papers have appeared in journals such as *Economic and Political*, Bombay, *Seminar*, New Delhi, *Studies in Humanities and Social Sciences*, Shimla, *Indian Literature*, New Delhi, and *Comparative and Continental Philosophy*, USA. He is also the author of *'Weeping' and Other Essays on Being and Writing* (2011) and *A Story of Political Ideas for Young Readers, Volume 1: Socrates, Plato, Aristotle, Machiavelli* (2010).

He has published three collections of poems in Hindi: the most recent collection was published by HarperCollins, India, in 2009. He has translated into Hindi collections of poems by the well-known Norwegian poets Olav Hauge and Lars Amund Vaage, and (with Teji Grover) *Hedda Gabler* and *The Master Builder*, plays by Henrik Ibsen, all published by Vani Prakashan, New Delhi. His poems have been translated into English, Telugu, Marathi, Swedish, Norwegian and Estonian.

He was invited to read his poems in the international poetry festivals at Visby, Sweden, and Ulvik, Norway, in 2008, in India Festival at Trondheim, Norway, in 2011, and at the Writers House in Tallinn, Estonia, in 2014.

Email: rustamsingh1@gmail.com